"In an age like ours, when people and groups claiming to be Christian do not ostensibly appear to look, think, can be nothing more important than centrality of Jesus for the life of the di claims his name. In this book, Todd H calls us to a recalibration of our lives t that we might be authentic witnesses in _ .............

**Alan Hirsch,** author of *Reframation* and founder of Movement Leaders Collective

"Like a horrific scene from a war zone, we are walking through the rubble of our failed churches. From here Todd Hunter speaks. Refusing to smooth over the grievous sins of the church, Hunter leads us steadfastly on a course to reconstruct our approach to church by going deep with Jesus, the founder and perfecter of our faith, the one constant amid the ruins of failed religion. A gifted thinker, compassionate pastor, and seasoned leader, Hunter guides us through our pain. For all those besieged by the hurts of a failed church, *What Jesus Intended* arrives at this most crucial of moments to be the balm for our wounded souls."
**David Fitch,** Lindner Chair of Evangelical Theology at Northern Seminary

"Reading this book feels like having a calm yet vital conversation with a wise friend. Recognizing how bad religion causes traumatic wounds, Todd Hunter does a great job of pointing us to Jesus and faith that heals. Like all books, this one uses words. But coming from Todd, they're not empty. In the thirty-plus years I've known him, he has consistently lived good religion and has shown what he is writing about. That's why I recommend this book, because in it you'll hear Todd's heart of encouragement, and you'll realize that you're not alone on your faith journey."
**Brian Doerksen,** songwriter and recording artist

"With compassion and humility, Bishop Todd Hunter offers a lifeline to the many people who have been hurt in and by the contemporary church, by inviting us to see with fresh eyes the person and mission of Jesus. As it turns out, Christ spoke against the 'bad religion' of his day and invited his original hearers, and us, into his kingdom where questions are welcomed, dignity is restored, and goodness is tangibly evident in our world and among our neighbors. If you're intrigued by Jesus but skeptical of the church, this book suggests you're in the right place."
**Katelyn Beaty,** author of *Celebrities for Jesus: How Personas, Platforms, and Profits Are Hurting the Church*

"It is easy to turn to tried-and-true slogans and excuses in an era when the church seems to be caught on the shoals of sexual, racial, and cultural failure. 'Aren't we all sinners?' 'There is so much negativity, we just need to be more affirming.' Trite solutions are often the result of a superficial diagnosis. Todd Hunter wisely and with unflinching honesty exposes the legitimate heartache and confusion felt by many who have departed the faith. He invites us, amid our struggle, to re-engage the wild, unpredictable, and table-turning Jesus whose kindness can comfort any suspicious and confused heart. This is a profound work of wisdom and love."

**Dan B. Allender,** professor and founding president of the Seattle School of Theology and Psychology and author of *Redeeming Heartache*

# WHAT JESUS INTENDED

## FINDING TRUE FAITH IN THE RUBBLE OF BAD RELIGION

### TODD D. HUNTER

FOREWORD BY ESAU McCAULLEY

An imprint of InterVarsity Press
Downers Grove, Illinois

**InterVarsity Press**
P.O. Box 1400 | Downers Grove, IL 60515-1426
ivpress.com | email@ivpress.com

InterVarsity Press® is the publishing division of InterVarsity Christian Fellowship/USA®. For more information, visit intervarsity.org.

While any stories in this book are true, some names and identifying information may have been changed to protect the privacy of individuals.

The publisher cannot verify the accuracy or functionality of website URLs used in this book beyond the date of publication.

Cover design: David Fassett
Interior design: Jeanna Wiggins

ISBN 978-1-5140-0495-1 (print) | ISBN 978-1-5140-0496-8 (digital)

Printed in the United States of America ♾

**Library of Congress Cataloging-in-Publication Data**
A catalog record for this book is available from the Library of Congress.

30  29  28  27  26  25  24  23  |  12  11  10  9  8  7  6  5  4  3  2  1

---

---

# CONTENTS

# FOREWORD

## ESAU McCAULLEY

**It is no stretch to say that we live** in complicated times. Many Christians are trying to make sense of what it means to follow Jesus in a fractured culture. We are often presented with two alternatives, neither of which is very appealing: deny the failings we observe within the church or contend that Christianity is not up to the challenges posed by our age.

I am not sure I still qualify as young, but I speak with younger Christians who are inspired by the vision of life presented in the pages of Scripture but struggle to find that vision take flesh in churches or in the lives of many pastors and clergy. They are dismayed to see that too many of our leaders seem to be more shaped by Fox News or MSNBC than the gospel of Jesus Christ. Wearied by the endless culture wars, they turned to Jesus hoping to find a better way—only to find the same talking points from outside the church following them inside it, the only difference being that our leaders evoke Jesus to give cover to principles derived from elsewhere.

It is a small comfort to know that in some ways we are like every generation of Christians, always in danger of falling into one heresy or another. The church is often tossed to and fro by the winds of culture. We are not unique.

Nonetheless, it is helpful to hear from Christian leaders who have direct experience dealing with the church's failings but have not lost hope that we can be better than we are. Bishop Todd Hunter has given us that in this book. As I worked my way through this book, I knew I was reading the reflections of someone who has asked the hard questions about the church's problems and come out the other side more committed to Christ than ever. The word *wisdom* is bandied about too easily, but that is good description for what Bishop Hunter has written here. It is a wise reflection on the person, work, and intentions of Jesus from someone who has spent his entire adult life in ministry, beginning in the Jesus movement of the 1970s to the present day.

The answers he gives to our problems are compelling precisely because of the simplicity and clarity born of long reflection. He points the reader to the person of Jesus, asking the most essential of questions: What were the aims of Jesus? What was Christ trying to accomplish in and through the church? Hunter suggests that by discovering those aims and letting Jesus' goals for us and his kingdom take root in our hearts, we can find ourselves and our vocations as followers of the Messiah.

According to Bishop Hunter, we do not need to remake Christianity for the modern person; the modern person needs to rediscover Jesus as the solution to the problems and traumas that plague humanity in every age. Do not misunderstand. This is not a closed-minded reaffirmation of old-time religion. Instead, Bishop Hunter explores the particular ways in which the aims of Jesus help us chart a path through our current malaise. For example, he asks how the intentions and teachings of Jesus help us deal with cynicism and despair. He wonders how Jesus assists in making sense of the evil done in the name of religion, or how the Messiah helps us wrestle with issues of identity.

Readers will not find solutions that allow us to set aside the difficulties that beset followers of Jesus. Hunter rightly notes that the full solutions to our traumas await Christ's second advent. Instead, readers will find fresh inspiration to take up again the Scriptures and the practices of the Christian tradition and find in them sufficient hope to finish the race that our Lord and Savior set before us. Hunter does not take us to a final destination, but he equips us for the journey.

# INTRODUCTION

*From the very first day, we were there, taking it all in—we heard it with our own ears, saw it with our own eyes, verified it with our own hands. The Word of Life appeared right before our eyes; we saw it happen! And now we're telling you in most sober prose that what we witnessed was, incredibly, this: The infinite Life of God himself took shape before us.*

**1 JOHN 1:1-2 MSG**

*Everyone was amazed. "What kind of man is this?" they said. "Even the winds and the waves obey him!"*

**MATTHEW 8:27 GNT**

**The surf was spectacularly high.** It was the kind of day that brought out the best, buff, bronzed-skinned surfers with their jealousy-inducing inlaid boards. I was not one of them. I idolized them. Because the waves were so high that day, and being young, I was bodysurfing, barely keeping my head above the sea's surface by treading water intensely.

I, and millions of other churchgoing people, have often felt the same way: swamped by church hurts, smothered by bad religion, we employ lots of intense effort to avoid drowning spiritually.

In the menacing ocean, my toes did not trust that my head's position above the water was sustainable. With a mind of their own, my feet became a GPS system—frantically recalculating their route as the churning sea ruled my body, commanding it to move in fitful directions. As each unsure, ungrounded moment passed—as if they had a brain—my feet, thrashing and pushing downward frantically, were questing: Where is the bottom? My feet were like a bodily expression of a spiritually troubled heart: Will I finally be overwhelmed by my troubles with faith? Is there a way out of this monstrous set of faith-killing waves washing over me?

In instants of spiritual trouble, I desperately need and look for a place to stand. I need some secure, solid ground that provides me the ability to maneuver out of my terrible, fearful disquiet. Experience had taught my boyish feet to believe in, rely on, and long for the safe, stabilizing sand of the ocean floor. My toes knew that sand contained the mental and emotional properties of *rock* on which a boy could make his stand against the primordial power of the ocean.

Today, the sand of faith seems not sturdy, shifting under the feet of faith-challenged people, making their spiritual stance unsure and insecure. Gallop says that only 31 percent of Americans have a "great deal or quite a lot" of confidence in the church. And that while confidence in the church has been slipping for many years, it went down 6 percent in just one year.[1] Furthermore, Gallop reports, "declines in formal identification with a religion, self-reported membership in a church, self-reported religious service attendance, personal importance of religion, and a decline in belief in God."[2]

Justin Giboney articulates the thinking of many people concerned about church:

> To be fair, we must acknowledge the injustices and sins that have caused so many to leave the church and rebuke Christian orthodoxy. They're rebelling against rules, wielded with prejudice and malice, that continue to bludgeon women and racial minorities. They're responding to structures that cover up abuses of power and morals that

are enforced discriminately. They're rejecting religious institutions that serve white supremacy, support misogyny, and mistreat same-sex-attracted people, all while claiming a biblical basis. Such harshness and hypocrisy have led to one of the biggest lies of our age: that a person cannot be orthodox—upholding historic Christian doctrine and morals—and also compassionate.[3]

The troublesome headlines of fallen leaders and bad religion, along with personal negative experiences in church, leave many so tossed about that they become de-churched. Victims of leadership malpractice and spiritual abuse in the church feel battered and carried away by contextual forces over which they have no say.

With similar reactions, many have found themselves in the path of the sexual, verbal, emotional, and other forms of abuse being uncovered in the church. They feel spiritual stress analogous to what I felt in the waters of big surf: fear manifesting itself in a racing mind of religious confusion, shallow breathing that ousts spiritual peace, a sky-high heart rate of churchly nervousness. In those moments we frantically search the surface of the water right and left for a spiritual friend bobbing along near us, for anyone or anything that could provide assurance that my bad religious experience could be survived.

## BOBBING ALONG TOO

Over a lifetime of faith, I have a few times been tempted to distance myself from, or even quit, religion and church. My wife and I, after spending decades in Christian leadership, had a period of a couple years we now affectionately call our "de-churched era." We tried several churches, but nothing healed our scars or fed us with hope for sustainable spirituality. The most consistent thing we could do in that era was to cling to the weekly fellowship of a small, contemplative home group focused on spiritual formation. These fellow seekers kept the thread of faith moving through the fabric of our life. But in hindsight I can see how easy it is for that thread to get yanked and pulled all the way out of one's life.

In the same way that two bodysurfers are in the waves together, you and I will be bobbing along together in this book.

I see you. I get you. I perceive you straining, spiritually, to keep your head above water. I see a similar, widespread reality in countless others via conversations I have had with religious leaders of all denominations who are profoundly discouraged with various aspects of the church. These people cover the organizational chart of church leadership: home group leaders, Sunday school and youth workers, pastors, administrators, women's and men's program leaders, members of vestries and boards, parish council members, professors and deans, and denominational leaders of every level. No category or type is immune.

## BAD RELIGION HURTS

Let's define a key concept. When I say *bad religion*, I do not have in mind the 1980's Los Angeles punk band by that name. I use the phrase as an imaginative and evocative way to represent the various ways things go wrong in church life.

Church hurts from bad religion are accompanied by a profound sense of loss. They hurt more than most of life's other hurts. They sometimes feel on par with divorce or even death. I know for me, church hurts were personal, deeply internal, at the core of my soul. Bad religion is confusing, depressing and sidelining. I sometimes wondered if I could survive church.

Happily, so far so good. I've hung on as a sincere follower of Jesus. But truth be told, messed-up religion has more than once pushed my face to the sand and held me under its power longer than I was comfortable, longer than I thought I could survive. Feelings of discouragement, despair, hopelessness, irritation, and even anger accompanied these moments. We sometimes fear we have given our hearts, our very lives, to something that, at net, is harmful to humanity. We wonder, similar to victims of abuse, if there is something wrong with us, that maybe we bring these things on ourselves. The sustained experience of bad religion is a complex, layered, nuanced harm.

I have real empathy for those who are deconstructing elements of their faith. Such eras of spiritual life can, once on the other side of them, lead to constructive growth. The progress of a pilgrim is always the goal of my spiritual life. I have pursued this progress by staying on the path marked by the person and work of Jesus. I have survived by constantly making my way back to Jesus, to the nature of his being, his words, and his works.

## A LIFE PRESERVER

The big idea of this book is that it is possible to survive the waves of bad religion. The round, orange life preserver I am throwing out is constructed by the aims of Jesus. There is, I have found, salvation by clinging to that which Jesus self-consciously pursued. When I have been bowled over in the turbulent water of bad religion, flailing and floundering, Jesus is the rock on which my spiritual feet have found secure footing. I continually seek to come back to him as the one about whom amazed disciples marveled, "What kind of man is this? Even the wind and the waves obey him!" (Matthew 8:27). Jesus' followers would later come to see that in him all the fullness of God was pleased to dwell (Colossians 1:19), and that he is the only one who has preeminence (Colossians 1:18), who is above all (John 3.31), who is teacher and Lord (John 13:13), who is "heir of all things . . . through whom [God] made the universe. [Jesus] is the radiance of God's glory and the exact representation of his being, sustaining all things by his powerful word" (Hebrews 1:2-3).

Jesus has sustained me. He is the animating source of my belonging to, and service of, the church. Nothing in the contemporary ills of the church should eclipse this truth: alignment to the aims of Jesus is fundamental to Christian spirituality. Pursuing alignment with the aims of Jesus is the path on which we discover good religion, find the true and good life, and become humanity as God intended.

## ABOUT THIS BOOK

The stories I tell about others in this book are real, emerging from real conversations with real people. However, to protect their privacy I have changed the names and contextual details surrounding the stories. In the telling of my own stories, I have done similarly. I narrate my real experiences without naming names or describing specific contexts that could inadvertently identify others.

The chapters to come will give a vision for and explain how I have kept my head above water as the deep disappointments of church life rolled over me. Come with me now as we talk straightforwardly about bad religion and the cure for it found in the aims of Jesus.

# 1

# AM I THE ONLY ONE WHO THINKS THIS?

## HOW THE CHURCH FAILED US

*[These religious leaders] tie together heavy packs that are impossible to carry. They put them on the shoulders of others, but are unwilling to lift a finger to move them. . . . [They] forget about the more important matters of the Law: justice, peace, and faith. . . . They look beautiful on the outside. But inside they are full of dead bones and all kinds of filth.*

**MATTHEW 23:4, 23, 27 CEB**

*Woe to you experts in religion! For you hide the truth from the people. You won't accept it for yourselves, and you prevent others from having a chance to believe it.*

**LUKE 11:52 TLB**

**Monica's parents were** relentless churchgoers. Only Christian music played in her home. Movies rated R were not just disallowed, they were unthinkable. Monica was raised on the power and goodness of love. And then, in her senior year of high school, her parents divorced in a hailstorm of violent verbal battles. Heavy weights of relational tension crashed into Monica's life, wrecking the joy of her graduation. Because the divorce was so expensive, going away to college was in jeopardy. She did okay-ish in the aftermath, finding posttrauma wisdom in counseling and in the consolation of friends who stuck by her.

Monica later married, only to have her husband leave for someone else who better satisfied his sexual peculiarities. The postdivorce response of her just-turned-teenagers was not as benign as hers had been to her parents. Acting out angrily at home, disrespecting school authorities, partying, and abusing substances followed. She could see that her kids were self-medicating, but they were so emotionally distant that she could not get through to them. She hoped the church youth group would help, but her kids were mostly judged and marginalized there, even by long-term friends, because of their reactions to their parents' divorce.

Next came years of exhaustion from being a single mom. Monica was constantly forced to decide between paychecks, her kids' daily welfare, and self-care. On a humdrum Tuesday evening in February, with the frail winter light receding rapidly around her, having fought the traffic home, she walked through the garage door into the dark kitchen to discover that the kids were out again without telling her where they'd gone. Monica spattered her keys impatiently on the counter, and flung herself, a depressed heap, onto the sofa.

The lights were off, and unknown to her, chill-inducing inner darkness was coming. In the next instant it was like someone pushed a button and blackout window shades came rolling down, thickly covering the openings to her soul, vanquishing the ability to see anything—including God.

Monica was hurt. She was in the grip of disappointment with religion. But she got up—she was tough—she always got up. She flicked on the kitchen light, ate some leftovers while streaming a bit of her favorite show, and went to bed hoping the kids were safe. She tried to morph *hoping* into *praying* but that button was broken on the back of too many dashed expectations.

## FACING CHURCH TROUBLE

Lord knows how many times I have tossed churchly keys and thrown myself on a couch of religious despair. I have felt the expansive loneliness of not being able to turn apprehension about the church into prayer.

I've been embroiled in the ups and downs of church my whole life. I know how religious sausage is made—both the ingredients and the process. As an insider to the church, I know all the yuck of what we are made of and how we fail to deal with it righteously. Despair, dejection, hopelessness, impotence, irritation, anger, and depression have knocked on the door of my heart with great persistence over a long period of time. To be fair, there are of course wonderful moments in ministry where we see lightbulbs of insight shine bright, healing come with its joy, and deliverance from evil relieve the victim and spread hope and peace to their family and friends.

However, viewed from any number of angles, the church is in oodles of trouble. Modern forms of media make it impossible for the church to hide her sins, her hypocrisy. The church's easy dismissal or even dehumanizing hate for those she deems to be wrong adds to her failure to look and sound anything like Jesus. Compelling or even plausible reasons to consider faith in Jesus and to attend church are, for many, hard to find. Jesus seems eclipsed by the dark shadow of bad religion.

That said, after long years working in the church, both sinning and being sinned against within her, I still believe in the body of Christ—the church. Why? Because I believe in Jesus now more than ever. Jesus summons and establishes the church, his body, the ones elected to keep the movement started by Jesus going.

I am captivated by Jesus' intrinsic goodness and his inherent wisdom, and by the fact that his power was always selflessly exercised for the good of others. I am motivated to embrace his movement by the notion that even right now he is living the most consequential life imaginable as he stewards humanity and all God's creation to its intended fulfillment. I find it stunningly compelling that he invites me, and you, and unchurched

doubters—with our sins, reservations, errors, and confusions—
to be in on that story.

## IT HAS ALWAYS BEEN THIS WAY

Messed-up church is the way it has always been. Church history
does not unfold like a series of ups and downs that one might
trace on a line graph: up at the resurrection, down at Doubting
Thomas, up at the church fathers, down at Constantine, up at the
Reformation, down in our day. No, the reality of church life is
that it unfolds like train tracks, protracted stretches of both/and,
of simultaneity, of good and bad religion all mixed up together
in local churches and in individual people.

The problematic elements in the body of Christ have been in
play since, with twelve close friends, Jesus roamed Nazareth,
Galilee, Judea, and Samaria. That band of followers, and the historic body of which Jesus is the head, has never been perfect.
Skeptical onlookers would have always had ample reason to
reject Jesus because of the close company he kept. Peter, after
protesting that he would never do so, denied Jesus. "There you
go," an onlooker might have said, "I knew Jesus' followers were
hypocrites!" Like angry marketing agents, whose message was
not cutting through the clutter, James and John wanted to call
down fire on whole cities who they deemed did not welcome
Jesus with enough enthusiasm. I can hear a skeptic saying:
"Christians are emotionally unstable and should not be trusted
with power!" Jesus washed the feet of Judas the deceiving be-
trayer, to which someone might respond: "Those friends of Jesus
are in it just for the pieces of silver they get out of it!"

The church does not need to be perfect for the purposes of God
to advance. But that is not an excuse for the church to be an agent
of darkness or abuse that forces unbelievers to grope for the
God who is actually very close. Perfection is not the goal—rather,

the goal is to be people whose lives suggest the plausibility of the Christ-story.

## DIFFERENT DETAILS, SAME EFFECT

My details are different—yours too—but chances are you and I have struggled in Monica's rough, dark-at-the-bottom water.

Many—lots, actually—of my clergy and lay leader friends, who once had vibrant faith, who served the church and cared for the needs of others, no longer participate in weekly worship. They remain good people whom I love. I enjoy their company. I can see that they maintain some sort of private devotion that is important to them.

But they are beaten down in faith, battered in heart, and bruised in soul.

The latest church scandal now seems to arrive, like Sunday football, every week. Some people follow all the muck and—dishearteningly to me—rank the scandals for us. For instance, I found the "Top 10 Evangelical Sex Scandals of 2021." The subhead line read, "The religion had a busy year!"[1] Most every list of "top religious news stories" of a given year contain at least one salacious story of a fallen pastor. For instance, in the short span of 2020 through 2022, we heard about Brian Houston and Carl Lentz of Hillsong, Ravi Zacharias, Jerry Falwell Jr., and Mark Driscoll. It is depressing in the extreme to hear the latest coverups of sexual abuse by high-ranking leaders in the Roman Catholic Church and the Southern Baptist Convention. One Midwest pastor was caught having had sex with a sixteen-year-old member of his church.[2] A megachurch pastor with a global following estimated to be between 1.4 million and 5 million people, pled guilty in Los Angeles to charges of sex with minors.[3] #ChurchToo has been in our face for a while now, which grieves those in the church who have a conscience.[4]

Outside the sexual arena, our faith-shoulders slump when we are given mental pictures of mass graves of indigenous children who died from neglect or mistreatment at the hands of the church.[5] In a unique form of Christian nationalism, leaders of the Russian Orthodox Church, including Archbishop Krill, are giving Putin's government core rationale for the war in Ukraine.[6] It is unthinkable that there is any justification for Ukrainian elderly, mothers, and children to be sacrificed for a false, utterly un-Jesus-like religious vision. Just before being *killed* they were under his *care*. His priests would have married the women, baptized the kids, and normally would have given last rites to the elderly on a deathbed in a quiet, spiritual home. Now they pray over body parts blown to bits by modern weapons of war—egged on by the worst of bad religion.

But that's just the news. Now it gets personal.

As a decades-long supervisor of pastors, I have had an up-close view of multitudes of fallen leaders, whose bad religion was manifest in extramarital affairs, drugs, alcohol, stealing money, spiritual abuse, abuse of power, and sexual harassment. Each incidence, considering the real trauma to victim-survivors, is a genuine heartbreak. Direct victims and associated victims are left spiritually bleeding in the wake of bad religion. Victims fear they have nowhere to turn to find healing, that if they become whistleblowers, telling their story, the church will revictimize them in order to protect its reputation.

Given all that, only about 22 percent of Americans attend church weekly.[7] And post-Covid church attendance is down 40 to 64 percent.[8] Over the past twenty years, average church attendance has shrunk from 137 to 65.[9] A new Gallop poll shows that belief in God in America is at an all-time low and that this downward trend is driven in large part by young people.

I read a recent article that dug deep into the phenomena of young people struggling with faith. The article stated that evangelicals in particular are losing their young in epidemic numbers. Young people "resent how politics has shadowed their relationship with God and believe that Christ's lessons of humility, tolerance, and love have been forgotten."[10]

The article noted that if young people can't ask honest "questions and get decent answers, they will bail" on church. One college student said, "Our faith, now synonymous with unwavering support for Donald Trump, is causing many to question how Christians could sell out women, immigrants, Black people, Indigenous people, people of color, the LGBTQ+ community and the poor for the sake of political power. . . . Gen Z sees the hypocrisy of Christians today." Another student said, "I've started to think of Christianity as causing more harm than good."

The article observed that listening is key: "Most young people don't care about religion, but if you have young people trying to grapple with their faith—so they can make sense of it, given the world they experience—you should listen to them."

One young man, who had dreamed of being a pastor since he was a child and had prepared throughout university for ministry, said that "over the last five years, I've done a 180- or at least a 90-degree turn, questioning traditional understandings of God."[11]

Among the larger adult population, only 40 percent of Americans believe God intervenes in human life in response to prayer. Just slightly more than a third of the people in the United States have confidence in the church. Americans are most confident in the military and in small businesses.[12]

Pastors not only experience this rejection and observe this shrinkage daily, they also feel it in their gut in two profound ways: (1) it is discouraging to work hard, with sincere love for others and see dwindling fruit; (2) it is disheartening to pursue Christian virtue only to have the church turn on you for some political reason. Sadly, forms of abuse flow both ways in church. Just ask any pastor who tried to guide a congregation through the

Trump years and the Covid-19 pandemic. Thousands of pastors, members of church councils and church staffs were hounded and hammered by congregations who could not agree about shutting down worship, social distancing, masks, or vaccines. Thirty-eight percent of pastors ponder leaving the ministry to work somewhere else.[13]

In spiritual darkness, with seemingly nowhere to turn, a bright red EXIT sign beckons, and for many church leaders, the church becomes a reality only in their rearview mirror. In moments when bad religion overwhelms the good, the incoherent confusion gives way to what seems a compelling path articulated by a pop-rock lyric from the 1960s: "We've got to get out this place if it's the last thing we ever do . . . 'cause girl, there's a better life for me and you."[14]

## TO EXIT OR NOT?

The temptation to exit church has gripped eras of my life like an irritating itch. *Just leave*, the thinking goes, *and the annoying, prickling stings will go away.*

When I was an adolescent, the liberal mainline church my family attended stripped Jesus of anything that made him real. They failed to attribute to him any difference-making power. This antipreaching almost killed my budding faith. It was like spraying spiritual Roundup onto my searching heart, which like a tiny shoot, was straining to break through the hard soil of ignorance and cynicism.

Religion is so infuriating in part because it contains incoherent confusions. I experienced this sad, clouding mixture in the Jesus Movement of the 1970s, in which I found faith in God. We were known for a lot of talk about and practice of love and grace, as well as the acceptance of my generation's particularities of attitude, mod clothing, and hair styles. This atmosphere helped us know for sure that God loved and forgave our sexual, drug, and alcohol sins.

The disconcerting confusion crept in when I discovered that this love did not extend to everyone. For instance, it was implied that our faction of the church had all aspects of Christian spirituality right. Our *spiritual movement* was not like those other corrupt *denominations* that had it wrong. Our interpretations of the Bible were dead-on. They contained no ignorance or bias, which meant they were filled with certainty that funded a less-than-humble, self-assured approach toward others. The smallest difference in doctrinal understanding could be weaponized in the war with the people we heard our leaders and teachers ridicule: individuals like Robert Schuller of the Crystal Cathedral or whole groups of people, like Roman Catholics or mainline Protestants.

Later I encountered the good, the bad, and the ugly of the charismatic and Pentecostal worlds. I have seen amazing miracles of healing and seen the aftereffect of people being delivered from evil. I have rejoiced with friends who received Spirit-empowered, life-changing insight from biblical gifts of the Spirit: words of knowledge, words of wisdom, prophecies, and discernment. Wow! Amazing!

Sadly, something else is simultaneously true: more than a few of the most anointed, Spirit-empowered people I have known were also highly manipulative, sexually immoral, and relationally unloving, and they secretly abused various substances—legal and illegal. I've observed leaders using spiritual gifts maliciously and slanderously in order get their way. I loved and admired the people I am here calling to mind. I frequently wished I were as spiritually gifted as them.

But this is also true: I don't think I have ever gotten all the way to the bottom of the crushing *personal* disappointment of their *public* falls from grace. Mulling the effects of bad religion,

I was reminded of the inner work of healing I still need from when the #MeToo Movement morphed into #ChurchToo. Churchly messes spilled into public for any open-minded person to see.

When these things happen, I again quickly imagine the EXIT sign as thousands more people give up on church, on religion, sidelining Jesus in their life.

Continuing my story, in the late nineties I participated in many conversations with young Christian leaders who were wrestling with issues of postmodernism. It is true that in some cases the church had wed herself too closely to elements of modernism that in hindsight were not helpful to spirituality in the way of Jesus. To the degree the church was unconsciously in the grip of modernity, a critique was undeniably called for. But along the way, under a withering criticism of truth that too often became cynical condemnation, I witnessed hundreds of leaders and thousands of Christian believers walk away from faith.

They lost their confidence that *there is a way that things are* apart from and prior to our sensual experience of them, our thinking about them, or the imperfections of the language we use to talk about reality. I get all that.

But it is fundamental to knowing Jesus that there is truth, and that humankind has access to it, even if that access is perplexing due to contextual factors, one's specific perspective, and the limits of language. If there is a Creator-God who is purposeful, wise, and loving, then there certainly is a way that things are. This means there is a truthful reality to be discovered, albeit in the partial way fallen humans see, as through a glass darkly (1 Corinthians 13:12). Thankfully, Paul's idea goes further: some day we will see the Creator-God of Truth face to face. Then our religious and spiritual knowledge will no longer be partial. We will know fully, even as God currently knows us and his whole creation fully. But we don't have to wait for that moment. We can move in that direction, for in Christ Jesus, God's sphere and God's time have broken into human history.

I grieve that so many of my friends, seeing the rationale for religion crumble around them, have bailed out on the reality that the trinitarian God is superintending history toward his good purposes.

Most recently my heart has broken almost to the point of despair as I've watched large portions of the church sell their soul to both wings of American partisan politics. Some, seeking rightful social change, have joined progressive causes that have become unhitched from the biblical story and biblical ethics, in favor of political paradigms and political practices. Love for Jesus and for enemy is not easily felt among this crowd. The failure to love gets justified by the frame of secular partisan politics.

But this is to lose our way, for anything *social*—persons, patterns, structures, whether broken or finding in-process redemption—comes from, belongs to, and is currently being supervised by God. God is always central. Social issues cannot be properly and fully understood apart from this divine perspective. Therefore, we cannot find full and proper divine justice apart from God working on his terms. The vision for social justice that arises from the narrative of Scripture cannot come to pass based on the chicanery of election cycles or the slanted bombast of cable news.

I have genuine empathy for the frustration associated with the reality that justice seems to always come at a snail's pace. I get the impatience that comes with slowness, with delay. But rejecting the person and work of God in and through his people is not the answer. Rejection of the God–human partnership will bring neither speed nor accuracy to issues of justice. It will result in pseudo justice on the terms of partisan politics, creating winners and losers that merely perpetuate our present cycles of hatred, condemnation, and dehumanizing of those in one's rival political party.

Others have lost their way at the intersection of right-wing religion and politics by joining a form of Christian nationalism. But *nationalism* can never be *Christian*. A Christian can care about their nation—and in a narrow sense be a *patriot*. But only carefully, self-critically, in a limited, restricted way, as a subset of joining God in his care for the whole world, the entire globe, and all persons, regardless of their nation, tribe, ethnicity, or skin color, whether such persons are stable-in-place or migrants, born in-country or immigrants. The old children's spiritual sings forth the truth of the matter: "Red and yellow, black and white, they are precious in his sight, Jesus loves the little children of the world." Joining Jesus in his love means we cannot restrict our love to our own nation . . . and call such love *Christian*.

My stories are of course multiplied by the millions in the varied experiences of others. Given all that, my keen focus is this: lots of people are losing faith, hope, and love as they react in real time to bad religion and the damage it does to the reputation of Jesus. I respect and love these people. I know from my own experience what it feels like to be personally harmed by churchly malpractice. I have felt the dark clouds of dejection that come upon a person when one witnesses harm to family and friends by the church. I know what it is to feel piercing depression when one sees, again, in the news the fall of a still another famous Christian leader.

Before us now, two roads diverge: one toward hope, healing, and restoration; the other toward bleakness, deterioration, and death. This book is written to gain a fresh hearing for Jesus, and to nudge us down the road to the renewal of faith.

## NOTHING HAS WORKED

My stream of late-twentieth-century evangelicalism was full of activistic leaders who wanted to, and expected to, change the world. We came of age in a time when churchly religion was good, not just barely tolerated. The church was gaining power in politics, education, and legislation. We fought for and won seats at tables with presidents, princes, and kings. But with the benefit of hindsight, we paid a huge price in lost street cred. We absorbed major dents to the reputation of the church and the plausibility of Jesus. We fought wrong battles, used erroneous tactics, and lost far more than we won.

It might be impossible, but for the education of it, give it some effort: try to visualize Jesus fighting culture wars by partnering with the political, social, and religious leaders of his day. We quickly see it is nonsense. It is so clear now that we should have modeled our private and congregational piety after him, not political consultants, who are experts in using people manipulatively—including the church.

"Sometimes I think we've advanced / but then I look at where we are."[15]

It pops into my mind in meetings, while driving, or mindlessly folding clothes. It sometimes troubles my sleep, the nightmare dogmatically refusing to stop. Nothing in my generation worked.

Some nuance: I know this statement is not factually true. Lots of good stuff happened because of the church in my lifetime. However, such good is usually quiet and receives no media coverage. Headlines and TV station news crawlers are reserved for stunning sinners.

If I know that is true, then why the pestering thought, *Nothing in my generation worked*?

We had Billy Graham crusades. The worldwide influence of C. S. Lewis. Church growth models. The megachurch movement. The charismatic renewal. Pentecostal movements. The homeschool movement. The proliferation of Christian schools and universities. The emerging church. Vatican II. Mother Teresa. The ancient-future worship movement. The missional movement. The Alpha movement. The spiritual formation movement. Protest movements.

Despite all that, we have the sobering, if not depressing, realities given us by Gallop and the latest disheartening headline about something sinful in the church.

I suppose identifying all this could just be my perfectionism at work, but I doubt it. I've seen the same reaction in thousands of others with all types of temperaments and with enneagram numbers all around the circle. Additionally, I know there is a counterargument to what I am saying: "Well, Todd, where would the world be without the good the church has done?" Right. I agree.

But at this moment, I am not relying on strict logic or calculating a set of religious debits and credits. I am concentrating our focus on a common feeling—the deep sensation of spiritual loss, of a real and pestering consciousness of religious despair. Countless church leaders have devoted their lives to what in their genuine experience was an intractable church and unyielding world. The church and the world seem worse off than when we started.

Many thousands of lay leaders wonder, *What's the point? We followed the pastor, fresh off the vision-casting seminar he and the staff attended, up the missional mountain, only to find that he was using us and actually did not care for our souls. But he was happy to compute our programmatic participation, count our attendance, and calculate our tithe.*

I know that is a caricature. So why bring it up? Because I have heard sentiments like those described above from far too many people. If we want to get to the heart of many disillusioned Christians, we need to ponder with honesty our worst fear: Maybe *God does not work?*

## REMAIN A CHRISTIAN?

As you got a peek into my story above, you may have wondered, *Todd, how have you remained a Christian, stayed in the church, been loyal to its institutional forms, and even continued to serve as a leader in the church?*

The answer is this: It may have taken me some time to do so, but in reaction to each of the deep disappointments described, I, all credit and thanks to God, had the foundational, unshakable instinct to always make my way back to Jesus, to his person, words, and works. It only takes a little effort to notice the spectacular pure beauty of Jesus, and, in becoming alert to his inexpressible goodness, to find meaning in and through Jesus for the rest of one's life story—the virtuous and honorable, the corrupt and the unpleasant.

Even if we desperately want to, there is really no place to hide with our church hurts and religious disappointment. If we stop going to church, we still drag our letdowns around like a bag of rocks. They still trouble our soul, driving us nuts like a car alarm that won't shut off. If we cut off people from our old life, we just add loneliness to bad religion. The vast majority of people who have left the church tell me the one thing they regret is the loss of relationships that were facilitated at church.

But by turning to Jesus in the way I suggest, something else happens that is rejuvenating: the Bible, even with all the controversy and doubt that surrounds it, becomes alive and beloved again. The pages of the Gospels become a pop-up greeting card, surprising us, confirming to us again the virtuousness of Jesus and thereby inviting us, if not compelling us, to find life and the meaning of life in him. And more: the letters of John and Peter present testimonies of what it was like to walk firsthand with Jesus, the real Jesus, not the Jesus battered by the long history of bad religion. I always wondered, Could the stories they tell and the ideas they communicate be determinative of

Christian spirituality, rather than the latest study showing the demise of church though shrinking attendance and the effects of bad religion?

It is such a pop-up moment that I hope for in this book—to gain a fresh hearing from Jesus by patiently listening to his aims, on his terms, in his words. In times of war, persons and property are bombed to bits. Occasionally we see a picture of a baby, a mom, or a young, brave, self-sacrificing soldier, or some artifact of cultural value being rescued from the rubble. My hope is to rescue the reputation of Jesus from the rubble of bad religion.

If we paused for a moment of honesty, each of us could enumerate and describe the ways and incidences in which we, individually, along with institutional forms of religion, collectively, have co-opted Jesus for our own biased, selfish, and broken aims, burying him in the wreckage of false spirituality. This book seeks to liberate our understanding of Jesus, to center him in the town square of our hearts and let him speak for himself, revealing his aims, and thereby giving the basis for, and calling us to, human life as God intended.

Monica still struggles with the church and the inconsistent effects it has on people—the truly good and the terribly bad. She recently told me that she is a little better, the shades have come up a bit. Her retreating darkness is giving way to swelling levels of light, revealing a morsel, a mustard seed of spiritual hunger. Small but real, it is a hunger she tells me she would like satisfied.

## EXERCISE
### APPLYING THE AIMS OF JESUS TO MY LIFE

1. Grief and sadness need time and space to rise to the surface and become noticeable. If you are ready, call to mind two incidences of bad religion in your life. They likely exist on a scale from direct abuse to the relational pain of being dismissed by work or church mates. Being gentle with

yourself, but challenging any fear, recall as much detail as you can. It might help you to journal or record a voice memo of what transpired in the incidences you name. Notice what your body is or has been saying to you. (If you are recalling incidences of severe trauma, be mindful and tender to yourself. If you remain traumatized, please seek help from a trauma-informed therapist, spiritual director, or pastor. What we are looking for in these exercises is small steps toward posttraumatic insight and spiritual growth. Such faith development is possible, but it takes patience and expert guidance.)

2. Now notice: in what ways was your faith injured? Loss of confidence in God, the Bible, or church? Cynicism toward Christian leaders? Do you feel lost in some way?

3. In his earthly life, Jesus clearly observed the practices and consequences of bad religion. Today he sees you. He sees the scars you bear in your memory, heart, soul, and social relations. His aim is your healing. Pause now to invite him to do so. Take the risk of opening yourself to the good religion of Jesus.

---

You might begin with this prayer:

*Jesus, I am a mixture of faith and fear, confidence and doubt—Lord, help my unbelief. As a first step on the journey away from bad religion I want to turn to the truth of who you are. I want to begin what I know may be the slow, halting pivot to your heart and your aims. I ask you to release me to a free and spacious place in which I am no longer bound by the sins of others.*

What words of your own would you like to add?

# 2

# CAN I FIND FAITH AGAIN?

## A FRESH PROPOSAL REGARDING JESUS

*This is my beloved Son, with whom*
*I am well pleased; listen to him.*

**MATTHEW 17:5 ESV**

*The reason I was born and came into the world is to testify*
*to the truth. Everyone on the side of truth listens to me.*

**JOHN 18:37**

*Keep your mind on Jesus. . . . Then you won't*
*get discouraged and give up.*

**HEBREWS 12:3 CEV**

**"No Christian leader has spoken to her like that in years."**

A ministry staff on the West Coast had become dysfunctional—like a bag of porcupines banging into each other, each sharp poke adding to relational injury. Five years before, they were a tight, dynamic team that had started and grown an effective, loving, and serving ministry of faith. They invited me to work with them to create a process in which they could discover what had gone wrong. These young people, now in their late-twenties had laid it all on the line, no sacrifice was too much. Until it was.

Our opening conversation revealed that over the past year or so they had been shutting down with each other and losing passion for their shared work. Communication was distant and dishonest in the sense that they feared whether they could still be real with each other. Could they still count on the innocence of their college days, back when they thought the best of each other? Drip by drip, their declining interrelations swelled to become a river carrying poor rapport and low motivation.

As we worked, we discovered a pattern at the center of the pain and disillusionment: mistreatment by the senior leader. They all had witnessed it and experienced it personally but didn't know how to name it or deal with it. They questioned what they were seeing: *Can this be real? Maybe I am the problem—maybe I am just becoming cynical and bitter? Am I overreacting? If I say something about the leader, who is a friend and gave me my first chance in ministry, is that an act of betrayal? Will saying something harm the ministry, maybe even tear down everything we have built together? Maybe ruin the guy's marriage?*

They had been drinking a powerful and toxic mix. Blended with needing to please the leader was a fear of his displeasure. Losing oneself to please a leader, and a leader using that people-pleasing impulse to his own ends, does not facilitate godly self-sacrifice. It is manipulation. It is a form of spiritual abuse. When a leader cultivates an atmosphere in which others fear him and then uses that fear to get his way, people do not submit in the good sense of giving one's self to a common cause—rather, they are subtly bullied into submission. They are victims of an abuse of power.

I know this is stereotypical, but I don't expect young men to break into tears upon hearing some obviously needed encouragement for their wives to enjoy some self-care. These tears sprang up in a conversation with the staff that included their spouses. I wanted to meet with spouses because mistreated staff cannot help but to carry their pain home. Sometimes, because couples are so devoted to Christ and ministry, spiritual trauma dominates life at home too. This is not healthy, but when we are in it, we can't see it. But it is revealed in statements like, "Geez, this is dominating our whole life . . ." And it really means just that: one's whole life is controlled, governed, and subjugated by pain born of one aspect of our life—ministry.

Frank and Terri were one of the ministry couples around the table at our catered chicken enchilada dinner—with awesome tomatillo-cilantro-lime sauce—in the small fellowship hall. They recounted their experience of terrifying moments after a serious cancer diagnosis. The emotions were still near the surface of their life. Two years prior, Terri, the outreach coordinator at the ministry, had a difficult series of chemotherapy and radiation treatments with a long hospital stay. After further complications and with her body weakening under the toll, the doctors monitored her closely. She could have died more than once over that six-month period. The flat pewter walls of the hospital were bright compared with the dark fear, anxiety, and depression coiling around Terri's heart.

Like any of us in that condition, she longed to be seen, to be understood, to receive compassion. But all she got from the leader and his in-circle was criticism for not coming back to work soon enough and for poor performance when she was back. She was regularly gaslit about being overly emotional. I say "gaslit" because much of the criticism was a cover for the fact that the senior leader had become emotionally dependent on Terri. When she found the time, the energy, the courage, and the clarity to look back, she could see a pattern of inappropriate talk and un-wanted touching. The leader begged her over and over, "Come back . . . I need you."

Terri was not seen. She was not understood. There was no compassion for how the cancer brutalized her body, and how the real possibility of death for her had scarred her soul. She was used to making the leader feel better, to meeting his malfunc-tioning psychological needs.

I was startled when Frank's face fell with a thud into his hands, tears squeezing out from his fingers. Looking up, his red face flush with emotion, he said, "Thank you . . . no Christian leader has talked to her like that in years."

All I had done was state the obvious: Terri needs care, some time off, and a space to process the abuse from her leader/friend/ boss. I am no hero. It did not take a genius to see that Terri needed and deserved an investment in her in the form of time to recuperate from the cancer treatment and the work trauma brought on by leadership malpractice. I just showed basic care. But when a leadership team is stuck in a cycle of abuse, the obvious is not always discernible.

In moments like I describe, leaders gain a fresh hearing for Jesus—and in that hearing find healing. Sometimes our voice becomes His voice. People recognize the love and truth in it. Jesus reemerges from the debris of bad religion. Hope is restored. The hurting get in touch with Jesus' aim to do them good. Sadly, these moments of refreshment are more and more needed as the church struggles to understand and deal with spiritual abuse, with abuses of power.

## THAT WHICH WE DON'T KNOW

There are things we know we don't know—and we acknowledge it. For instance, most of us know we cannot name from memory all the books of the Bible, in chronological order. Most of us would have to admit that we are not fully confident of our ability to carefully articulate the relations of the Trinity or describe the human-divine nature of Jesus or how the virgin birth worked or to precisely name the programs and mechanisms of hell—or heaven for that matter. We know in our guts that it is tough to explain how an ancient set of writings is "the Bible" and thereby authoritative for all things Christian. We know our limitations on these topics.

But it gets worse: sometimes we don't know what we need to know. Case in point: It had never crossed my mind that Jesus had aims. Athletes and sales managers have aims, but didn't Jesus merely come to die? I had been taught that his death had aims—namely the forgiveness of my sins so I could go to heaven when I die. But in the conduct and practices of his daily life— Jesus had aims there too? I could sense that this idea had the potential to expand, and thereby improve, my knowledge of and followership of Jesus—to wake up an important aspect of Christian spirituality.

Unless we come to see that there is more to the Christian religion than being let off God's angry hook and having our sinful slate wiped clean—as vital as those are—we will never receive the life from above that Jesus aimed to give us. Sin, guilt, forgiveness, the cross, resurrection, and the afterlife are certainly core and important aspects of Christian spirituality, but they are not its only qualities. The key feature of discipleship to Jesus is to learn to be, do, and say as he taught was best—and to do it as the overflow of love for God and neighbor.

Jesus is a real person, alive today, and we can indeed learn from him. And, in contrast to the church, he is doing well. He is always redemptively on the move in the world. We are invited to enter a real relationship with precisely this Jesus—and in making his aims our own, to be an agent of healing in the church and redemption in the world.

Tom Wright and Ben Meyer introduced me to the aims of Jesus.[1] Reading their work had a destabilizing, deconstructing effect on my walk with Jesus. But it was a good destabilizing. It was like cutting open a fresh bag of Legos and dumping out on the table the pieces of what would transform into a Lego model. It looks at first like a scattered mess. But as one carefully follows the instructions, piece by piece, Lego bits become a complete and attractive sculpture. I know: I recently received a birthday gift of

LEGO bricks and turned sixteen hundred pieces of various shapes, colors, and sizes into a 911 Turbo Porsche.

Or imagine the moment you pour jigsaw puzzle pieces from the box onto a table. Most of us begin sorting the scrambled, jumbled pile by finding the flat pieces and constructing the frame for the rest of the puzzle. That is what the kingdom aims of Jesus did for me. They gave me a new frame for all the other pieces of my life and for all the fragments of religious thought that move around in my heart and mind.

As I discovered the aims of Jesus, I wondered, What would this breakthrough call for? What amendment of life might be necessary? What in my followership of Jesus might be better upon this discovery? Would coming to see the aims of Jesus make me a better servant? Other hope-filled questions also came to mind: Would embracing the aims of Jesus as my own lead to a beautiful, radiant life that others experience as for their good? Would I become a whole person, not always battered by the worst aspects of my life? Would my disordered desires find healing and reorientation around the aims of God in Christ? Living in alignment with the aims of Jesus, might I, please God, become an agent of healing, justice, and reconciliation?

The revelation of the kingdom aims of Jesus was not merely new or fresh, it was exhilarating. I felt like a pearl merchant who had found the pearl of greatest value. I did not just want to think about the aims of Jesus or talk about them, I wanted in on them as a recipient and an ambassador. I wanted Jesus' aims to become mine. I was—and am—willing to change anything to align my life with the aims of Jesus.

## HYPOCRISY: THE FACE OF BAD RELIGION

Nolan was skinny and tall for his age, and his pile of wavy red hair stood out noticeably above other students walking the hallways of his university. By day, he was must-see entertainment under the cool shade of the bell tower. At night he held court, legs hanging over the side of a gray sofa in the common area of the dorm. Nolan was noted for being a clever and humorously sarcastic persecutor of faith and pesterer of the faithful. If the topic was religion—and especially Christianity—few challenged him. His playful hyperbole was a reliable hoot.

As a professor on campus who taught courses on how people come to faith and grow in faith, I caught wind of Nolan's legendary status. I asked a fellow student to give me his email and then asked Nolan to meet me for coffee—in my case tea. After checking me out through a few students who had taken my class, he agreed.

As we sat, I noticed obvious intelligence and childlikeness on his countenance. I was especially curious and motivated to get to know Nolan because his friends had told me that in his *performances,* he was really wearing his heart on his sleeve. As we began to talk, he admitted it, saying, "I am not trying to deceive or pretend. I am just a bit of a ham, an outgoing actor-type who is also a verbal processor."

As our conversation passed through the awkward come-to-trust-you phase, Nolan cautiously revealed a bit more. "Mocking heaven and hell," he told me, was "the public revelation of internal strife." He said he had no clear idea about what happens to someone—their body, soul, consciousness—when they die. "I just think of devils in red felt suits and people rotating on a spit and roasting like marshmallows for all eternity is a funny spoof." Moving to another topic, he told me, "Because I am bugged by it, I love calling out the toxic combination of religion and politics." On a bit of roll now, he said, "but I also grapple in sincerity with what it means to be a truly good person and how to participate concretely in social angst and political turmoil. I really cannot imagine how humanity can fix itself and organize itself in healthy ways that are good for everyone, every type and class of people."

I had been warned that hypocrites were to Nolan what a rodent is to a hawk: prey. When I asked him about why hypocrisy was such a big deal to him, he recounted a story that gave rise to him feeling troubled about the inconsistency he noticed between what he believed about life and, like the church members he enjoyed skewering, his actual ability to live in alignment with those beliefs.

He told me that his dad died young from a stroke that doctors said could have been prevented with diet and exercise. After describing his desire to avoid his dad's fate, he said "I know gut-bomb burritos and beer are not health food. But . . . I don't know . . . they taste good in the moment!" Staring down at his watered-down iced latte, Nolan speculated aloud, "Does that make *me* a hypocrite?"

I maintain sincere appreciation for Nolan. He was genuine. There was un-self-conscious humility in Nolan that kept him from being unlikable as he processed out loud his skepticism about Christianity. At bottom, I think he was fumbling for insight, for perspective.

## A FRESH PROPOSAL

I have a proposal. It can enliven and shift conversations. It pleasantly surprises people, the way wine aficionados speak about the finish of a certain wine, or the way a salsa enthusiast praises the slow burn of their favorite pico de gallo.

Let's set the proposal forth by pondering with an open mind a set of questions; roomy, heart-opening, mind-expanding questions:

- To what was Jesus conscious as he lived, taught, and did kingdom works of power?
- What did he think the Father was doing in and through him?
- What were Jesus' hopes, dreams, purposes, desired outcomes, goals, and ambitions—his aims?

If we can get anywhere near answering those questions, we will find refreshment for our own faith and gain confidence for helping others renew their faith and grow as followers of Jesus. The conscious aims of Jesus have real explanatory power and are not easily batted away. They penetrate barriers and work in creative ways on the imagination. They are experienced as personal, not doctrinal. They contain the power of invitation, of discovery.

### COME TO ME

As Nolan and I noticed the time and were about to get on with our afternoon, I wanted to leave him with a hopeful, forward-looking thought. "Nolan," I said, "if born of respect, or even better love, for the thing sought, questioning is a common means of honest seeking, of spiritual growth." I relayed to him the truth that after decades of faith, I still have questions pressing on my mind, troubling my heart, pulling at the part of me that sincerely loves God and others. It is usually only with hindsight that I recognize that my searching led to discovery. I wanted Nolan to have that hope.

Jesus often interacted with people who, like you and me, given their confusion about religion, asked tough questions. In Jesus' day, such people were unsettled because everything happening in and through Jesus seemed to contradict what they previously believed about the religion in which they were brought up. To them—to us—Jesus generated and held open an appealing relational atmosphere for seeking good religion among the bad:

> Come to me, all you who are weary and burdened, and I will give you rest. Take my yoke upon you and learn from me, for I am gentle and humble in heart, and you will find rest for your souls. For my yoke is easy and my burden is light. (Matthew 11:28-30)

Even with or maybe precisely because we have doubts and questions, notice the basis for Jesus' invitation to follow him: his gentle and humble character. Seeking renewed faith would be impossible if Jesus were indeed the caricature of bad religion: mean, dictatorial, arrogant, and abusive. But he is not. Over thousands of years, billions of people have sought him and found him to be what he claimed to be: tender and calm, humble and meek.

Those adjectives attributed to Jesus can also describe the feelings associated with renewing one's faith in Jesus. We too can search calmly and seek with humility within an overall disposition of desiring to learn about Jesus. This is what Jesus makes clear with his analogy of a yoke. A yoke is a wooden instrument that is attached to the necks of two animals and then fastened to a plow or cart, which together, in lockstep, the animals pull. By this analogy Jesus is giving hope to those who have felt abused by misguided religion. The spirituality of his day was often heavy, loading people down with toxic forms of religion. This misguided spirituality contaminated faith-seeking. It built barriers to God, not bridges.

Jesus wanted people to know that seeking after him could occur in his easy yoke, with us tied closely to him, in a relational vibe distinguished by its unforced rhythms of grace—nothing heavy or ill-fitting but something free and light (see Matthew 11:28-30 MSG).

Being yoked with Jesus, though unimaginable while in the disorienting fog of their church reality, would have been a healing balm for Frank and Terri. It would have torn off that which bound them to bad religion. It would have taken that which handcuffed them to spiritual abuse and joined them instead to the Healer, the Restorer, the Guide—to good religion.

## OPENING TO JESUS

A few weeks after my meeting with Nolan, walking to the dining hall to get some dinner before my evening class, I passed him on the sidewalk. After a quick "hello" he told me that, although he was not yet ready to answer, he was beginning to hear a question from Jesus spring spontaneously to mind: *Who do you say that I am?*

## EXERCISE
### APPLYING THE AIMS OF JESUS TO MY LIFE

1. How does it land with you that Jesus has aims into which he invites you? What are the specific church hurts or disappointments with God that make it difficult for you to accept the invitation of Jesus? In hopeful contrast, when have you welcomed and experienced the invitation of Jesus in a way that led to a deeper, more robust faith? Is there anything about those experiences you can draw on in the midst of loss and doubt?

2. How are you doing with the question, "Who do you say that I am?" What is clear to you? What excites you? What concerns you or holds you back? I invite you to make space to sit with Jesus, to practice listening to his heart, to see what comes up.

3. Give some thought to the areas you are or are not currently involved with in the church. What do you see as your responsibility in the midst of a dysfunctional church? What power or agency do you possess and need to name? How might you use that muscle to take steps to fresh faith and help others do the same?

You might begin with this prayer:

*God, I want to hope that there is good religion. But given my church hurts, I am fearful, reticent. Placing hope in church seems unrealistic, daring, maybe naive. But I open myself now to a fresh hearing of Jesus. I do so with the hope that you will heal me and that you will renew my faith.*

What words of your own would you like to add?

# 3

# I AM FAILING TO CONNECT TO FAITH AND CHURCH

## JESUS' SELF-IDENTITY IS OUR RESCUE

*I and the Father are one.*

**JOHN 10:30**

*I have come down from heaven not to do my will*
*but to do the will of him who sent me.*

**JOHN 6:38**

*I love the Father and do exactly what my Father has commanded me.*

**JOHN 14:31**

*I have come into the world as a light, so that no one*
*who believes in me should stay in darkness.*

**JOHN 12:46**

**Aubrey—quiet, but easy to be with—**was a friend of a friend. I occasionally bumped into her at social events for mutual colleagues. She knew I was a Christian leader, and I had reason to believe she volunteered at her church. Neither of us had ever broached the topic of religion.

On a sweaty July evening, we found ourselves at a birthday party for a coworker of mine, who was her roommate. After presents were opened, "Happy Birthday" sung, and cake served, some guests, carefully balancing their plate and drink, snaked through the crowded, stuffy dining room to find their way to the large front porch. Passing over the threshold, a soft evening breeze greeted us and brought audible sighs of relief.

I noticed Aubrey on the white slatted porch swing, leaning back against a teal lumbar pillow, red flip-flops dangling from her toes. Looking around, I noticed the only open seat left on the porch was on the low concrete wall that defined the porch. I sat there perpendicular to the swing, cup at my side, plate on my lap.

Aubrey turned to address me: "Can I tell you something?"

I wondered what might be coming but mustered up enough social confidence to blurt out a bouncy, "Sure!"

"I've lost motivation to go to church—and I wonder what that might say about me."

"Why, what's up?"

"My mom made us go to church up through high school," she said. "Mom thought that church attendance was the best way to make important social impressions. It meant you were at least trying to be a good, decent, moral person. Our family knew we were far from perfect, but we believed it was weird to not attend church. We were suspicious of those who did not go."

She went on: "Since I had to be at church, I tried to find something to truly believe in, something that would deeply ground my life, something bigger than me, able to calm my fears and satisfy my spiritual longings—something that would make sense of the seeming randomness of life, the hardships of life, the mysteries of life. I really wanted to connect Jesus, faith, church, and real life."

Aubrey went on to reveal that whenever she tried to discuss these things, her leaders tried to force her questions, feelings, and desires into certain, predetermined doctrinal boxes. Her church was all about right thinking.

She was rolling now, telling her story: "It's not so much that I rejected the boxes being offered me or the content of them. My setbacks in faith came because no one seemed to care about what was outside the box: me, my life, the world. I tried a few times to point out this disconnect, but it inevitably caused tension in my relationship with leaders.

"I got labeled as stubborn and difficult because I would not contort myself enough to fit the box. No one ever seemed to notice the power of the rigid lines that formed the box—how unyielding and dehumanizing they felt. I was never shunned, but people I hoped would become friends-in-seeking grew edgy when I raised questions. Over time, they became distant. Now, I want to be distant from the whole church. I mean, how strange is it that ideas are preeminent, while a hurting, seeking person right in front of your face is screened out because they have errant religious values?"

I felt it, so I said it: "I am so sorry, Aubrey, I know religion can seem insider, defensive, out of touch, and irrational."

A moment of silence passed, and sensing that she was leaving space for me, I asked, "After the experience of not being seen or heard by church leaders, what are your thoughts and feelings now—how has it affected your relationship with God?"

Aubrey, lifting her chin and turning again to look at me, said, "I realize that no matter what my mom intended, and no matter how blown off I feel by the church, I have been an honest, childlike seeker my whole life. I still seek God. I just no longer want to seek through the church."

When I asked if anything would make her reconsider church, she said no. And quickly added, "But I will never stop searching for God."

## THE REVELATION OF GOD

I have a bad habit while visiting museums. No, I don't climb over ropes or break rules and touch stuff I shouldn't. But I can get keenly involved in reading the plaques and watching explanatory videos, seeking the background of something: Who made it, who owned it, how was it passed down, how did it come to be in a museum? I suppose there is nothing wrong with my thirst for education. Except this: I can miss the thing itself. I might spend five minutes reading or listening to the audio headphones museums provide, but then I walk away having only given a glance at the actual display. The mind has been stimulated, but the eye has not taken the object to heart.

Sadly, this frequently happens with Jesus. He can be talked about, deconstructed, analyzed, and critiqued, and all the while we may miss the thing itself—in this case the person Jesus himself.

The apostle Paul sometimes writes like he has a pastor's hat on: "I pray that the eyes of your heart may be enlightened in order that you may know the hope to which [Jesus] has called you, the riches of his glorious inheritance in his holy people, and his incomparably great power for us who believe" (Ephesians 1:18-19).

First notice the phrase, "the eyes of your heart." Paul is differentiating between mere cognition or intellect and a deeper, spiritual, heart/soul knowing. Paul's pastoral prayer has an evangelistic overtone to it: he wishes that his readers would receive spiritual enlightenment. "The eyes of your heart" might sound like sentimental or mystical rhetoric, but Paul has concrete things he hopes the eyes of our heart will grasp: hope, calling, inheritance, and God's great power.

Paul Baloche's well-known worship song gives us the proper response to what the apostle Paul is praying will happen to us:

Open the eyes of my heart, Lord

Open the eyes of my heart

I want to see You.[1]

This chapter explores the idea that Jesus was deeply aware of who he was, why he mattered, and how his life both worked within and was meant to change human life, to be the shining example of humanity as God intended, the exemplar of the good religion we all seek. This truth comes gently through seven "I am" statements in the Gospel of John. These statements were uttered during conversations, in the context of the complexity of real life, the whole range of human experience, from brutality to beauty. These "I am" statements of Jesus are among the most direct insights into who Jesus thought he was and how his person and work—his aims—were meant for the good of others.

Hearing Jesus self-identify brings us back to the thing itself and draws our attention away from the nuttiness that often surrounds it. This approach does not absolve the church or deny bad religion. It just means that reports of bad religion are like winter ice on a windshield: distorting, if not completely obliterating, one's view. It takes a bit of effort, but using an ice scraper brings physical reality into clearer view. Jesus' "I am" statements work the same way. There is a bit of effort needed to take them in, but once we do, we see clearly how Jesus understood himself, that to which he was conscious, that which he thought was important, and that which constitutes good religion.

Unless we specifically consider this Jesus, explained in his own words, we will have missed the whole point and will likely fall into, or worse yet, become perpetrators of bad religion.

God is not distant or detached, nor is he a set of propositions to be grasped by people who belong to the upper crust of spiritual giants. He is not a concept to be explained by philosophers in cold terms like *unmoved mover*. Such thinking reduces religion to intellect, to our brain. Jesus' descriptions of himself are warm and practical. They reveal something of his person.

As we work together now, you will come to see that the ways Jesus referred to himself display exquisite incarnation through a deep bowing to earthly, daily, bodily human realities.

## I AM THE BREAD OF LIFE

Jesus said, "I am the bread of life" (see John 6:25-59). He did so in the context of explaining the meaning one should derive from the feeding of the five thousand. That miraculous moment of provision was a sign meant to point to the God-sentness, God-centeredness of Jesus. It was meant to show his power—a power greater even than Moses in the story of God feeding Israel with manna from heaven.

Having been filled with material goodness provided by Jesus, the astonished crowds go looking for him. However, when they find him on the other side of the sea, Jesus is not impressed with their motivation. He says they are seeking him for bodily reasons, for physical bread. Jesus tells them, "you shouldn't be working for perishable food, but for food that will last to eternal life—the food which the son of man will give you, the person whom God the father has stamped with his own mark."[2]

Jesus knows that though life in our physical body is important, most fundamentally we are never-ceasing beings. This insight alerts us to a most profound question: What substance is needed to sustain undying spiritual life? What Jesus is giving, and what we are meant to take of him into our lives, meets the spiritual needs of persons-as-souls who will live forever. The food that sustains eternal life is not a thing, but a person. Such sustenance comes from belief in and followership of Jesus.

In this story we see that Jesus' greatest concern was for people with spiritual hunger.

The challenge of the passage comes from the realization that our most cherished earthly blessings will not preserve our lives unto eternity. The promise is that, although we are starving beggars, those who feed on Jesus, who partake of him, will always be sustained and will never die.

Pondering Jesus' words brings to mind a comment from someone I once had in a small group of church people who were struggling with faith. I could see on Rob's countenance that he was striving to be straightforward.

He said to the group, "I know there is a humility and letting go of the world that is core to Christianity. But I need to admit that I feel the pull of a BMW, of keeping up with consumer tech trends, of owning a home with a pool for my kids. I also seek significance like that enjoyed by astronauts or surgeons or CEOs. I would like those things. I think it would feel nice, and they would give me markers of achievement. It seems to me that having stuff is a superior life than living paycheck to paycheck on a meager budget. Living like that is frustrating to me: why can't I have the good stuff, the good life? I think it would be cool to drive an awesome sports car!"

Rob continued, "In Christian spirituality, there is no equivalent to a BMW. A great car is a sign of arrival—there is nothing like that in church. Church doesn't have any way of telling you that you have arrived: like achieving different-colored karate belts or a getting a call up to the big leagues. There is no path to navigate that gets you the key to the executive suite. In Christianity, it seems to me, the rewards are hidden behind a veil. They come in another life. In this life we are left frustrated, desires out of reach, seeing through a glass darkly."

I think all of us around the table could empathize with Rob, at least to some degree. To find good religion we need to occasionally hear Jesus reminding us to not work for food that spoils, but to grasp the one on whom God has put his seal, stamped with his own mark. God's seal of approval on Jesus and his way of being, his values and priorities, is a major key to good religion.

Jesus knew that the Father had sent him with power for the precise purpose of meeting the deepest needs of humanity, needs that cannot be met in any other way. This is love. This is generosity. It's grace, kindness, and compassion. Eating the bread of life is the nourishment that produces and sustains good religion.

## LORD, GIVE US THIS BREAD

What mattered in the story of the feeding of the five thousand was not so much what Jesus did—the sign, the plaque to the side of an ancient museum piece—but to whom the sign pointed: to Jesus, to who he really is. The sign was meant to lift the crowd's eyes, to assist them in entering the story of Jesus' identity and what the Father was doing in and through him. It was meant to transport them from the world of mere bread, and the material worldview it represented, to the actual world of heaven, the realm of God, that had come to earth in Jesus, who was the true bread of life.

John 1:1, 14 says Jesus is *the Word* come from God to humanity. It came not haphazardly, but to accomplish something of God's purposes. The act of feeding the five thousand was a form of speech—a revelation. It was direct communication from God. So too were Jesus' explanations and teachings that surround the sign. This revelation had implications: it called for a decision, for a change in heart in which one would see Jesus, standing right in front of them, as *bread*. In the same way that bread is the basic, fundamental provision of life, so Jesus is the source, meaning, and purpose of life. Food is good, of course. It is fundamental to material life. Jesus is fundamental to the unseen, eternal life—which is the principal part of you, the foremost part of the human story, the biggest thing happening right now in the whole cosmos.

It is one thing to talk about Jesus, but for people like Aubrey, talking about Jesus happens within a framework of angst about the church, about religion, about hypocrisy, about tone-deafness, and about what is deemed to be the overpoliticization of the church. Boy, do I empathize.

For de-churched people, it sometimes seems as if the church specializes in causing us to miss Jesus. It brings spiritual courage to one's heart to know that the miracle of the feeding of the five thousand, and Jesus' statement that he is the true bread of life is meant to move us from church hurts to a prayer rising in our hearts: *Sir, give us this bread and don't ever stop!* (John 6.34 CEV)

That prayer not only keeps us from missing the thing itself but also welcomes *The Bread* into our lives—heart, soul, mind, emotions, will, and body. The Scriptures are chock-full of the idea of *eating the bread that God is giving in Jesus*, of seeking God, of pursuing him:

- You can't worship two gods at once. Loving one god, you'll end up hating the other. Adoration of one feeds contempt for the other. (Matthew 6:24 MSG)
- Seek first the kingdom of God. (Matthew 6:33 ESV)
- You will seek me and find me when you seek me with all your heart. (Jeremiah 29:13)
- O God, you are my God; earnestly I seek you. (Psalm 63:1 ESV)
- Seek the LORD your God and you will find him, if you search after him with all your heart and with all your soul. (Deuteronomy 4:29 ESV)
- I seek you with all my heart; do not let me stray from your commands. (Psalm 119:10)
- Blessed are those who hunger and thirst for righteousness, for they will be filled. (Matthew 5:6)

For Jesus' other "I am" statements, space does not allow the kind of exploration we just did concerning "the bread of life." But I want you to at least see how Jesus' self-conscious aims are articulated in these statements. They work like a powerful salve. They can ease the pain many experience in indecision, deconstruction, or skepticism. Well—at least they can if we let them speak for themselves, on their own terms, with an open mind.

## I AM THE LIGHT OF THE WORLD

Jesus was conscious of being the light of the world (John 8:12). To a world lost in darkness, Christ offers himself as a guide. Jesus could do this reliably because he is the original and eternal source of light in the universe. But he is also light for us who are spiritually blind by birth. As Billy Graham put it, "What the sun is to the earth, Jesus Christ is to the human heart."[3]

We had our carpets cleaned recently. I was surprised to see the young technician come in holding a black light in the form of a flashlight. When I asked him about it, he told me it was how he spotted dried pet urine that would otherwise be invisible the un-aided eye. It revealed the nasty truth hidden microscopically in the carpet fibers. His process was not just "yuck!"—it was the first step to being clean, fresh, and sanitary.

The light of Jesus is rescue from all the places where darkness traps us. It is salvation from disordered desire and addiction. Life of any kind cannot exist apart from light. Jesus' light is the source of hope—as is often said, hope coming from the light at the end of a scary tunnel.[4]

## I AM THE DOOR OF THE SHEEP

Jesus said, "I am the door of the sheep" (John 10:7, 9 ESV), sig-naling to the crowds that he was a protector from the harsh and frightening elements of life. His followers were often vulnerable people; coming from a society in which sheep and shepherds were common, they would have immediately got Jesus' point: shepherds protect their flocks from predators. During the night, when animals and thieves use the cover of darkness, the shepherd lays in the opening to the pen, keeping the sheep safely in and prowlers securely out.

Jesus knew he was providing the sense of fulfillment that comes when one knows their needs are the priority of the one in power. Jesus' priority is you. He not only laid down his life on the cross once and for all, but he lays down his life as protector every day. Security provided by Jesus, the door, is a reality anyone can enter.

## I AM THE GOOD SHEPHERD

Referring to a similar aspect of his conscious being, Jesus said "I am the good shepherd" (John 10:11, 14). Sheep cannot not exist without a shepherd. Wolves, wild dogs, and thieves would kill or steal them. Or the sheep would wander off.

To those people who have wandered away, the fretting reaction of the church feels like judgmentalism. It only makes things worse. Rather, Scripture invites the church into quiet confidence that the Good Shepherd is constantly seeking those sheep who couldn't stand church any longer. Jesus was keenly attuned to the notion that he, by the plan of God, was enlarging the flock to include Gentiles. Gentiles were *the* others, *the* outsiders of the long story of Israel. Jesus showed that they were no longer the enemy, and that he had come as the Savior of the *whole* world.[5]

No one, not even the one most understandably cynical about church, is excluded from the love and embrace of the God revealed in Jesus. Neither are occasional sinners, the barely religious, or those fleeing the church. The church can rest in God's longing, searching embrace of the Good Shepherd—and a core aspect of that rest is ceasing judgmentalism and adopting welcoming love.

## I AM THE RESURRECTION AND THE LIFE

The safety and security provided by Jesus—the Door and the Good Shepherd—extends even to death. Jesus is deeply aware of what death is, how it entered the world, and how it was being defeated in his life, substitutionary death, and bodily resurrection. Jesus knew he was dying and rising in our place to free us from sin and death. This is what he meant when he said, "I am the resurrection and the life" (John 11:25). Death, the biggest and final fear of humanity, is not the final word for those in Christ.

Jesus interacts with our real problems and pain not with religious moralism's "you should not have gotten disconnected—I told you to hold my hand!" Rather, Jesus comes to us as resurrection: "a new part of God's future . . . bursting into our present time, into the mess and grief, with good news, with hope, with new possibilities."[6] This is the confidence we can have for those struggling to reconnect to faith.

## I AM THE WAY, THE TRUTH AND THE LIFE

The social and mental landscape of Jesus' day was filled with religious claims and counterclaims. Into this reality Jesus spoke the words, "I am the way and the truth and the life" (John 14:6). Jesus was consciously aware that he was the source of all truth and knowledge about God. Jesus is the accessible path, the illuminating truth, and the giver of life for us who are lost, unaware, and dead without him.

What Jesus is saying here is not arrogant boasting or mean-spirited exclusion. It is generous inclusion based in a uniqueness necessary for such hospitality. It is one thing for an auto mechanic to offer to do brain surgery; it is another thing for a brain surgeon to make the same offer. Jesus is simply saying he has special capacity, and that his special capacity is being used to show humanity the way to the good and true life. God has acted decisively, particularly, and specifically in Jesus. This is not of first importance a negative comment on other religions—though that can be inferred too—it is primarily a positive claim about the unique ability of Jesus to guide us down the path of life, to be a model of humanity as God intended.

Life's path includes scary segments, especially when one is questioning the fundamental things of human life—like one's God concept. Jesus is simply stating a fact he knows to be accurate: he is the *way* down the path; he is the *truth* about whether or not you should try to cross a swollen stream; he is the way to *life* at the end of the trail of our existence.

## I AM THE TRUE VINE

Within Jewish tradition, the vine was a picture of Israel. With the words "I am the true vine" (John 15:1, 5), Jesus is saying he is the true Israel, Israel as God intended. And further, by attaching ourselves to Christ, by remaining in him and belonging to him, we enable His life to flow in and through us. In so doing, we become humanity as God intended.

In this picture, Jesus, the true vine, never goes away. He is stable, central, core. And this vine holds forth a generous, life-giving invitation: *abide in me*. Attach yourself to me and you will find life and the spiritual fruitfulness you have envisioned for your life.

This is the hope we have for the Aubreys in our life: they might have moved, but the True Vine remains steady, always inviting us and them to reattach to and abide in him.

## WHEN BREAD BECOMES *BREAD*

"I awoke sensing something was different." Lori was describing to me the moment her husband died. She had been sleeping on a recliner next to him when the moment came when she could no longer hear him breathing. Gordon, Lori's husband, had endured an exhausting, monitored, IV-filled life before succumbing to renal failure.

Lori had left her career as a corporate accountant to care for Gordon. When it was clear he only had a couple days to live, Lori organized a living wake in which Gordon, only semiconscious, was able to experience beautiful exchanges of love, capped by the moment his four-year-old granddaughter, Ari, placed her large stuffed unicorn into the bed, saying, "Here Grampa, Uni is here to help you feel better."

Soon after Gordon's death, Lori faced an unexpected challenge. She had heard about the reality of stages of grief and the need to pay attention to them, but she never imagined hidden, unprocessed grief spilling over in anger toward people she cared about.

Knowing she could not cope on her own, Lori convened her three best friends for a weekly dinner party on Friday nights. The first few dinner conversations were all about Lori, the pain of losing Gordon, and seeking to help her reconcile with those she had hurt while in her own pain and exhaustion as a caregiver.

Soon, her three friends noticed that they too had hidden hurts and strained relationships. Over the ensuing weeks, they began conversations of four-way mutual help. Word of this healing group got out and people wondered if they too could come.

About this time, as Lori was praying about what to do, she believes she heard the Lord speak to her, "Open your dining room." But Lori did not have a dining room, only an eat-in kitchen. As she pondered, she realized that she had an old dining set in the basement. Another thought quickly followed: the third bedroom in their small house, which had been converted to the hospice space where Gordon died, could be used as a dining room.

She recruited some help to carry the dining set upstairs, set the former bedroom up as a dining room, and started to include the others who had asked to come. They managed to squeeze eight people around a not-large table, filling the room to its walls. The cramped dining room became, locally, a legendary space in which guests were able to say aloud their deepest spiritual concerns. The new dining room and the firepit on the patio became thin spaces in which God was easily noticed in the midst of honest and safe conversation and mutual prayer.

When I asked Lori to look back on the experience, to tell me what she most noticed, she said,

"The dinners were remarkable occasions for experiencing and observing human transformation. Looking back, I realize we have become a family, one that chose ourselves as a way of healing childhood trauma that had followed us into adult life. We feel that we are being healed and released into closer followership of Jesus."

She finished her story with that look people get in their eyes when their brains are somewhere else. A brief moment of silence passed between us, and she said, "There is a wall-hanging in my home that captures a bit of what we came to call Friday Night Light":

In this house we forgive freely,

we love openly,

we have too much fun,

we make memories and we do life together.

The dinners are ongoing. Bread is facilitating moments in which the Bread of Life nourishes the souls of seekers.

## EXERCISE
### APPLYING THE AIMS OF JESUS TO MY LIFE

1. Slow yourself down. Recalling your experiences, when has God, Jesus, or the church been used as a means to someone else's end, hurting others in the process? As you consider the ways Jesus has been misrepresented, contrast that to how Jesus thought of himself. In so doing, what is most encouraging to you?

2. As you considered Jesus' self-identity, what came up for you? Which "I am" statement is currently most difficult to believe, to hope in? Which "I am" statement feels like a balm? Can you name what you feel and give thanks to God for it?

3. What might you do in coming days to water that seed of healing? Consider incorporating movement or the arts into that healing (walking, nature, music, painting, etc.).

---

You might begin with this prayer:

*Jesus, I am heartened by your stable self. I would love to fully trust that the qualities of your being are what is most real,*

*most determinative in the world. But I find you hidden behind*
*so much of what claims your name. Nevertheless, I now open*
*myself to a revelation of who you know yourself to be—for me,*
*for the world.*

What words of your own would you like to add?

# 4

# I'VE LOST THE RELIGIOUS PLOT LINE

## JESUS KNEW HE WAS LIVING IN AN UNFOLDING STORY

*This has all taken place that the writings of the prophets might be fulfilled.*

**MATTHEW 26:56**

*Today this scripture is fulfilled in your hearing.*

**LUKE 4:21**

*Everything must be fulfilled that is written about me in the Law of Moses, the Prophets and the Psalms.*

**LUKE 24:44**

**In 1978 I was in Bible college.** The New International Version of the Bible (NIV) was just getting popular. But my denomination, thinking it to be the sole reliable translation, was deeply committed to the King James Bible (KJV).

I didn't think it at all controversial at the time, but I had noticed that the NIV was easier for me and my friends to read. We found it more relatable, and thus got more out of it. When the head of our denomination came to visit one day, he held an informal conversation with the students, inviting us to ask questions. I related my experience with the NIV and asked what he thought. The response that followed was a ten-minute lecture on the orthodoxy of the KJV and the liberal evil of the NIV.

I was totally put in my place. Religious authority towered over my need to find in the Bible a plot line in which I could be an actor, a participant with Spirit-given agency of my own.

That moment was one of my first peeks into the narrowness and intractability of religious systems and their tendency to lose the plot in debatable details. This religious obstinacy is easily experienced as rejection, as being dismissed, as being considered stupid, and thus as not being valued.

Ironically, at the time of the publication of the KJV (1611) it was known as the first people's Bible. Its readability was meant for widest possible distribution. But under the power of centuries of tradition, it became a sword by which one could cut a line between so-called liberals and conservatives.

My first reading in the NIV helped me to see the story of the Bible, to not get stuck in words or verses or sentences, and thus to not lose its plot line. I had an instinct that I could not prove at the moment, but that has grown over the years: joining Jesus in his story is fundamental to Christian spirituality.

### I'M DONE

"Dad's in . . . way in. But I'm done."

Rory was done with church not because he felt bitterness toward others. It was from a sad recognition that, while he had some ideas about what he was supposed to believe, he did not know how to live. He had no clue about a story in which he could find a place for himself that seemed suitable to who he was.

We were sitting on the concrete bench to the side of our apartment tennis court, toweling off sweat from a match in which the younger, stronger, faster Rory had beaten me soundly. As I began to hear his story, the joy in his victorious body language was giving way to a distance and detachment in his eyes.

It was awkward hearing Rory talk about his dad, but we could not talk about Rory's issues of faith without the conversation involving his father.

Rory's father is a pastor. Not a megachurch pastor, but his long career at an influential church in a midsized town gave him megavisibility and mega-authority in the social, political, and ethical life of Rory's hometown. Rory loved his dad and from his childhood happily participated in the life of the church.

Rory's church was high on doctrine, big on clear theological thinking, keen on getting things right. Theological purity was the highest named value of the church. It animated the spiritual and social vibe of the congregation. Other churches were known for inspiring music or civic outreach programs, but this church was known for straight thinking about the Bible—verse by verse. Which meant for Rory and many others, the overall story of the Bible got lost.

As near as Rory could tell, arranging various Scriptures from the Bible into doctrinal statements was the core practice of Christian spirituality. In this way Rory came to see the Bible as something like Google or Wikipedia: you search its diverse statements for answers so that a Christian could navigate the various aspects of life—from cradle to grave.

Such an approach, though helpful from time to time, left Rory with big questions: *Who am I? What does it mean to be human? What am I supposed to do once I grasp all the right answers? Is there a livableness to Christianity or just intellectual apprehension of ideas? Is there a story for me to participate in?*

Churches and stories like Rory's are common, and they are understandable. Rory's dad grew up in a home dominated by religious experience that frequently became untethered from the Bible. People said bizarre things and partook in strange practices. This wounded his conscience, causing him to make a passionate inner vow to reform the church's beliefs and forms of worship by tying both tightly to statements in the Bible. It is hard to blame him. Unfortunately, Bible-thinking, when it is experienced as detached from real life, as well as from the story the Bible is telling and inviting us into, is also a common reason people say they are done with church.

This was true of Rory. He was not reacting, as was his dad, to something in the past. In his family and at church, he simply experienced the Bible as an encyclopedia of ideas—an approach that left him without a story to inhabit, a narrative to embody, and a whole picture though which he could make sense of all the complexities of his life: personality, temperament, gifts, inclinations, visions, body, sexuality, goals and desires, heart, emotions, thoughts, soul, and spirit.

With only Bible fragments rumbling around in his head, with nothing to form the bits of his life into a coherent story, Rory began to feel increasingly adrift: first from himself, then from others, and finally from God and the church.

## THE WILL OF MY FATHER

The overall purpose of Jesus' life, that which gave meaning to the story he was living, was to do the will of his Father. His specific aims were attached to and flowed from a relational reality: the Son to his Father. That is the model of Christian spirituality. Having its orientation in God, it draws us out of self-preoccupation. Over time, a Jesus-shaped, grace-based focus on God and others suctions the poison of church hurts, draining them into the kindness and care of God:

- My grace is sufficient for you, for my power is made perfect in weakness. (2 Corinthians 12:9)
- He will wipe every tear from their eyes. There will be no more death or mourning or crying or pain, for the old order of things has passed away. (Revelation 21:4)

Living without the aim of Jesus to do the will of God makes us feel exiled, cut off from something important. This explains in large part the common religious angst: *there must be something more.* Religion can seem stifling. In stark contrast, the life Jesus lived—and is living—was interesting, energizing, expansive, and vividly significant. We are invited into his present life.

We assume that top leaders like presidents, CEOs, and generals have aims. But Jesus? Didn't he just come to earth to die? Ben Meyer's *The Aims of Jesus* helps us to see that "for the man with aims, the non-drifter, aims are the man. They throw a flood of light on his history and they are the key to his historic selfhood."[1]

Meyers continues, " The key to [the] historical understanding [of Jesus] is the grasp of [his] intentionality, i.e., [his] perspective and purpose."[2]

Alignment to the aims of Jesus is the clearest ENTER sign and the most powerful motive for entering his story.

## AN INVITATION TO THE JESUS STORY

Jesus could have looked at all the bad stuff in the Old Testament (Adam and Eve's rebellion, Abraham's lies, the people grumbling against Moses and Aaron, David's adultery, etc.) and rejected the story those Scriptures were telling. He did not do so. He risked his whole being to place himself inside the story. Why? His confidence was in the fact that the story of Israel, even with its hard-to-understand low points, was being told by his Father. His trust was in its Author, the story itself, its plot line, its grand purpose. This allowed Jesus to be confident and present to the low points of his life as an agent of salvation, healing, and deliverance.

Eugene Peterson helps us see this:

The story of Jesus doesn't begin with Jesus. God had been at work for a long time. Salvation, which is the main business of Jesus, is an old business. Jesus is the coming together in final form of themes and energies and movements that had been set in motion before the foundation of the world.

Matthew opens the New Testament by setting the local story of Jesus in its world historical context. He makes sure that as we read his account of the birth, life, death, and resurrection of Jesus, we see the connections with everything that has gone before. Fulfilled is one of Matthew's characteristic verbs: such and such happened "that it might be fulfilled."

Jesus is unique, but he is not odd.[3]

I'd like to draw your attention to four words above: *connection*, *fulfilled*, *unique*, and *odd*. These words set an imaginative stage and draw us into alignment with the God-story—each one of us in our distinctive, irreplaceable way—uniquely ourselves, but not odd. God-designed variety is a feature of his creative intention. Let's see how these key ideas work together to restore our sense of God's story and our place as actors within it.

**Connection.** Church leaders commonly experience their work as disconnected from something truly transcendent. Human beings know deep in their being that life is supposed to matter, that it is supposed to unfold in a manner that surpasses mere chance, that includes happenstance, but also makes meaning of it. "In Jesus," Peterson says, "we see connections with everything that has gone before." The varied bits of *before* are the long, wide-ranging story of the Old Testament. That story gives shape, direction, and meaning to the life Jesus lived. In Jesus, *storiedness* gave *nowness* its essential character.

Without connection to the God-story, told from Adam and Eve to John the Baptist, Jesus' life would have been torn from its rightful context. Without connection to the story of Jesus and the apostles, our lives are torn from their native framework. Human beings are not merely composed of and defined by demographic descriptors: age, skin color, ethnicity, gender, sexual orientation, and economic class. Religion without an interpretive frame and spirituality without a coherent story in which we participate are two of the great winds that blow people away from God, religion, and the church.

*Fulfilled.* Most people have a profound instinct that their humanness is supposed to matter. We crave the knowledge and joyful confidence that one's life is attached to something meaningful. Feeling that our lives are merely dangling in the midst of unpleasant contextual factors we cannot control—economy, political eras, social tensions, traffic, and unlikable coworkers—we grasp at things we hope will fulfill us.

This grasping rarely goes well. Medicating bad feelings and the deep existential pain associated with being unfulfilled often drags people to the so-called big sins—the ones that get all the press: drugs, alcohol, pornography, affairs, addictions to life online, consumption of goods and experiences. After a while such habits of life get wearying. We tell ourselves they are fulfilling, but at some point, we recognize the truth: they *empty* life—they do not fill it. That which fails to medicate us also poisons and destroys families and friendships. Sins meant to medicate individuals fracture communities. After seeking relief through sinful habits and experiencing their predicable failure to provide true peace or joy, people who have considered themselves to be religious react with some mixture of frustration and shame. Shame is a common rationale for dropping out, for quitting church.

*Unique.* Fitting into the biblical story is not confining. It is not destructive to one's distinct personality. You get to stay your unique self—just with your sinful bits chiseled off by the Divine Sculptor. Story, and one's place in a story, is liberating. God's story is the specific place we are meant to find deliverance from all that binds, traps, and deceitfully snares human life. The story into which God invites us is like the gap in an otherwise closed window through which a trapped bird flies into freedom. God's story does not make cookie-cutter automatons. The creativity of God, revealed in his story, is limitless. Living out your specialness does not have to include fighting against God. The personal uniqueness we experience can be embraced and lived with enthusiasm and joy:

For you created my inmost being;

> you knit me together in my mother's womb...
> I am fearfully and wonderfully made . . .
> I was made in the secret place . . .
> I was woven together in the depths of the earth.

Your eyes saw my unformed body;

> all the days ordained for me were written in your book
> before one of them came to be. (Psalm 139:13-16)

The psalmist also gives a vision for one's life being filled with meaning—for being substantive in a way that is both satisfying to us and good for others, for all creation:

When I consider your heavens,
>  the work of your fingers,
the moon and the stars,
>  which you have set in place,
what is mankind that you are mindful of them,
>  human beings that you care for them?

You have made them a little lower than the angels
>  and crowned them with glory and honor.

You made them rulers over the works of your hands. (Psalm 8:3-6)

These two psalms alert us to a crucial and overarching fact of human life: *there is a givenness to it.* God created humans for a purpose (Psalm 8). But that givenness is not a mental, emotional, spiritual, or relational prison. On the contrary, God's purposes also create limitless variety that gives each human being a proper, unarrogant, nonnarcissistic sense of being special, of having freedom to express their unique characteristics (Psalm 139) within the overall narrative God is bringing to pass.

**Odd.** Jesus was unique. Eyewitnesses to Jesus' words and works of power often reacted like this:

> When Jesus concluded his address, the crowd burst into applause. They had never heard teaching like this. It was apparent that he was living everything he was saying—quite a contrast to their religion teachers! This was the best teaching they had ever heard. (Matthew 7:29 MSG).

> When the people saw the mutes speaking, the maimed healthy, the paraplegics walking around, the blind looking around, they were astonished and let everyone know that God was blazingly alive among them. (Matthew 15:31 MSG)

But within this distinctiveness Jesus was not *odd* because his life was lived within the unfolding plot line of God's story. His truth-illuminating teachings and matchless miracles flowed from his intense desire to fit into the plan of God. Jesus, sensing his unique role, wanting people to see that it was not odd in the sense of being outside the God–Israel story, said of his life, of his manner of being in the world, "Don't suppose for a minute that I have come to demolish the Scriptures—either God's Law or the Prophets. I'm not here to demolish but to complete. I am going to put it all together, pull it all together in a vast panorama" (Matthew 5:17 MSG).

At his unjust arrest, Jesus explained to the onlookers, "This has all taken place that the writings of the prophets might be fulfilled" (Matthew 26:56).

After the crucifixion, explaining those dark moments to a couple of his depressed followers who did not yet grasp the reality of the oddness, the total one-off-ness of the resurrection, Jesus explained it in terms of a story being fulfilled, which came as a huge surprise: "Beginning with Moses and all the Prophets, he explained to them what was said in all the Scriptures concerning himself. . . . Everything must be fulfilled that is written about me in the Law of Moses, the Prophets and the Psalms" (Luke 24:27, 44).

Jesus was never against Jewish law—the instructions for right living that God gave to his people in the Old Testament (Matthew 5:17-19). He came to demonstrate what true fulfillment of the law looked like. Jesus is not fighting *with* leaders as much as he is fighting *for* outsiders, *for* the purposes of his Father that were being thwarted by bad religion. Jesus' words criticizing religious leaders are motivated by concern for God's will. They reveal compassion in that they are spoken in consideration for those beaten down by bad religion.

The way some leaders pursued religion meant that they unintentionally worked against the purposes of God. They were judgmental, often angry at those who would not bow to them. They were proud and felt superior to others. This made them demean others and be heavy-handed. They were obsessed with creating and maintaining their image. Their passion was to be seen as more holy, strict, and zealous than others.

To find analogies in our culture, we might consider *famous fallen pastors*. Mostly men, these church leaders are successful at brand creation and management. Though publicly seeming to have it all together, these religious leaders are often secretly broken in heart and soul. They are driven by disordered desires that conflict with their doctrinal thoughts and spiritual pledges. At some point their desire to have the person, substance, or thing they crave overwhelms their stated public commitments. The power they amass to themselves through their public persona becomes the muscle they use to sway others to get their illicit needs met.

If God's story were likened to a melody, we would say Jesus lived in beautiful harmony with it, not gratingly out of tune. He is indeed the *way*, the *truth,* and the *life* (John 14:6). Being connected to God's story—seeking to fulfill it in our small but ordained ways—is meant to lead to unique, not odd lives. Our highest and best selves, created in God's image, will give us appropriate distinctiveness without the neurotic need for self-conceived, selfishly insisted-on ways of standing out from the crowd.

## RIVAL STORIES

Some people have a hard time detecting the intersection of God's story and their daily life. For others, however, there are more serious challenges with the ideas we have been discussing. For example, some people don't want any restrictions on their lives. Lots of us don't like being told what to do or think. We want to write our own story, thank you very much! I've been talking about God's story as large and inviting—granting us room to run. But some see this plot line as a confining boundary. They do not see that while plot lines give definition and meaning, they also give acres of freedom, space to run, and opportunity for self-expression.

I am trying to cast the vision that without story, life is fragmented and cohesion goes missing. This is what I was fearing and is what gave rise to my Bible school search for a translation that felt more welcoming. And Rory was reacting to the overuse of proof-texts that buried rather than revealed the story of the Bible.

Relying merely on verses of the Bible or favorite quotes from cherished leaders is like trying to stand on ice at warming polar caps, each fragment melting under one's feet. Soon there is no place to stand, no ability to be a self, no grounding for a life. Without God's story we deteriorate as we stoop to lesser purposes in our religious life, such as defining, defending, and protecting my denomination—or nondenomination. We try to prove that the beliefs of one's religious group are superior to all others. In every generation, some have co-opted Jesus into current politics. *We either use Jesus for our purposes or we find purpose as we follow Jesus into the story of God.*

The second tension has to do with the context in which we try to hear a new story and make meaning of life within it. For Americans, this calls to mind *America*—that powerfully evocative word that symbolizes an all-encompassing idea and a powerful force field that sucks into it all the elements of our lives. If we are not diligent, *America* can dwarf every other idea in our mind and take too much space in our hearts.

The language of *heritage* is often used to describe the historic uniqueness and greatness of America. We are constantly reminded that we are the best nation on the earth. Along this same line we are often reminded that we have had a *legacy* handed down to us. Implicit in the reminder of inheritance is the underlying command that we must protect and preserve it. Sometimes this calls forth benign forms of patriotism. But we need to make sure that God Almighty, the world's one, true Creator Lord, does not become "a character in the national story,"[4] rather than as it should be: Americans as characters in God's story.

Growing from a particularly vigorous form of American pragmatism, religion has often become a means to national ends. Among many reasons, this is true because the founding vision for America, and for democratic capitalism overall, requires a vaguely moral but not zealously religious people. For instance, peaceful transitions of political power require people to be moral enough to vote rather than kill. Commerce necessitates a populace ethical enough to produce and purchase goods, rather than be lazy or steal.

If American democratic capitalism required a vaguely moral and compliantly religious people, then society was going to need chaplains to bring such a people into being and keep them aligned with the goals of the nation. Chaplains to democratic capitalism, in the view and hopes of civil powers, ensure that citizens behave well in terms of politics, retail consumerism, and our system of debt that props up our purchasing power.

*Christianity as chaplaincy* to a nation or a political ideal of any sort (socialism, etc.), lacks the clarity, the compelling nature, and the vision and values and aims of Jesus. The thing to note here for our work is that when Christianity is reduced to being chaplains to a society, we are only allowed to dispense religion in small enough doses to not rattle political and economic powers, while being asked to foment high-enough religious potency to keep people in line with the values of public institutions. For individuals trying to follow Jesus, such a scheme is (as my mother, avoiding swear-words, used to say) *bass ackwards*.

## FREEDOM

A world-famous American distinctive that sometimes works against the story of God is its focus on finding and cultivating freedom. As individuals we are anxious to create a unique self, and we fear that outside influence might become soul destroying. We find it particularly uncool to conform to another person or power. Rather, we love autonomy. We value being self-determined individuals. We think it best and right that we should find within ourselves our truest selves and then act upon that discovery.

In American culture, freedom has been usually defined with a strong sense of permissiveness attached to it. We chafe against ethical norms, moral models, and religious traditions. This makes us into "an immediate society, without past and often without future: people who live utterly in the present and seek instant gratification."[5] That state of being will not facilitate following

Jesus into the story he was living. We rarely wonder, Once one is free from what is deemed to be restrictive religious traditions or churchly expectations, what will replace them as a basis for determining what is good for human flourishing?

But what if questions of purpose are of more value and precede questions of freedom? What if the divine invitation is "figure out *my* purpose for humans, for societies, and their structures; for economies and their systems of production and consumption; for bodies, for gender, and for sex—and then be as free as you would like to be!"

The conscious aims of Jesus were derived from the purposes that emerge from the story of God. That story is the interpretive key to knowing the true good, for living the truly good life, for finding meaning and human flourishing, and for living in harmony with God.

Without the guidance of the aims of Jesus, much of what is left in supposedly free human interaction is produced by the brutalities of self-interest, which of course can never honor God or serve neighbor or love an enemy. As Jesus said, "You can't worship two gods at once. Loving one god, you'll end up hating the other. Adoration of one feeds contempt for the other. You can't worship God and [national or individual interest] both" (Matthew 6:24 MSG). Jesus further said, "Worship the Lord your God, and serve him only" (Matthew 4:10).

## STORIED FLOURISHING

When we first met, Rory did not have the words handy on his mind, but over the course of our conversations I came to see that he was seeking that for which many burned-out, de-churched people long: a story that glues together the broken bits of life, that makes sense of human tragedy and beauty, evil and benevolence, heartbreak and healing.

Even trees have a story.

For many years I took a monthly retreat day at the Mission San Luis Rey in Oceanside, California. My cherished spiritual director lived in Oceanside, which made it convenient to see him too.

Inside the inner courtyard of the mission, surrounded by hundreds of rosebushes and manicured lawns, is a massive Peruvian pepper tree. A sturdy, black wrought-iron fence now protects the historic tree. On the top rail hangs a plaque that reads, "The oldest pepper tree in California was planted by Father Antonio Peyri in the middle of the mission garden. The seeds were brought to San Luis Rey in 1830 by a sailor from Peru and the tree still stands today."

I am not a big tree guy, but I love that tree. Arriving in the early morning for my retreat, in order to facilitate a time of contemplation, I would grab a chair from the nearby patio and set it under the shade of the tree. Settling into the chair, bringing myself to stillness and quiet, I would notice the robust and diverse life being sustained in the ecosystem of this ancient tree. Bees buzzed all around it. Insects of other sorts moved on and among its thousands of long, thin leaves. Its heavy, weeping branches were roads for squirrels and both hunting grounds and rest stops for several species of birds.

Each month, as I sipped hot chocolate in the cool coastal morning, that timeworn, twisted tree told me a story: we too are in an ecosystem that is divinely created, sustained, and being supervised to its God-initiated fulfillment. The first time I heard the story from which the aims of Jesus grew, I knew I would become an evangelist for the aims of Jesus. They reveal life-changing truths:

- There is more to Christian spirituality than examining individual leaves and the microbiology that give them color, shape, and life.
- The trees of our lives have particularities, but such quirks are in service to the whole.

- Branches downed by storms do not facilitate life as well as those that are livingly connected to the tree.

Rory, like most burned-out church people I have met over the years, was a decent human being, more honest than most, more willing than most to expose the longings and fears of his heart. He was just looking for what the pepper tree provided: a story that would sustain a meaningful life.

I want Rory and all my barely-hanging-on-to-faith friends to know that life, with all its mysteries and imperfections, its ambiguities and criminalities, has meaning that will, in the end, fulfill the purposes of God. I want those hurt by the church to see how the revelation of God in creation has, from ancient times up to now, called forth worship and obedience:

Lift up your eyes and look to the heavens:
> Who created all these?
He who brings out the starry host one by one
> and calls forth each of them by name.
Because of his great power and mighty strength,
> not one of them is missing. (Isaiah 40:26)

I want the spiritually depressed to be cheered by what the psalmist declares: "The heavens are telling the glory of God; they are a marvelous display of his craftsmanship. Day and night they keep on telling about God. Without a sound or word, silent in the skies, their message reaches out to all the world" (Psalm 19:1-4, TLB).

I want those who are understandably skeptical to consider Paul, striving for people to enter God's story, making the case that "since the creation of the world God's invisible qualities—his eternal power and divine nature—have been clearly seen, being understood from what has been made" (Romans 1:20).

Unspoken truth is articulated everywhere. I heard it in a pepper tree. Month by month, from its strong, steady, stable presence, there grew in my heart the possibility of finding and living in God's story, the story that animated the life and aims of Jesus.

## EXERCISE
## APPLYING THE AIMS OF JESUS TO MY LIFE

1. Is there a story about a particular people group, institution, or faith group that you have recently come to see differently? How did you feel when this revelatory truth unfolded? In what ways did you wrestle with God? If you believe there is an overarching story unfolding for the mutual flourishing of the whole world and all its people, where do you sense the Superintendent of that story inviting to you to participate?

2. Are there rival narratives you have been pursuing that keep you from living wholeheartedly in God's unfolding story? Name two of them and consider these questions: What is it about those stories that keeps me more loyal to them than God's story? What is keeping me from abandoning them in favor of the story of God?

You might begin with this prayer:

*God, I have felt all over the place the last few years. Everyone is telling me alternative stories—stars, politicians, social media, and commercials on TV. Those stories attach themselves to something wayward in me. I am sorry that I have gone missing and have abandoned the plot line.*

*But I see you again. I perceive your story. I hear your voice. This moment I rededicate myself to you, consecrating my whole life to your specific, beautiful, and redemptive story.*

What words of your own would you like to add?

# 5

# I FEEL PAIN, CYNICISM, AND DESPAIR—WHERE IS JESUS?

## JESUS' ORIENTATION TO THE KINGDOM OF GOD

*Do not be afraid, little flock, for your Father*
*has been pleased to give you the kingdom.*

**LUKE 12:32**

*I must proclaim the good news of the kingdom of God*
*to the other towns also, because that is why I was sent.*

**LUKE 4:43**

*[Pray] your kingdom come.*

**MATTHEW 6:10**

*Seek first the kingdom of God.*

**MATTHEW 6:33 ESV**

**"Nothing ever changes—not really."**

Martina's classmates were surprised to hear her speak out in our classroom. Teaching a course on evangelism, I was explaining the fact that Jesus' primary orientation for his life had to do with something he called *the kingdom of God*—the rule and reign of God.

Martina was not having it. "It doesn't seem like God is *ruling* anything to me. It seems to me that persistent human chaos, evil, and violence *reign*." To Martina, my teaching that the rule and reign of God was present and active seemed religiously *nice*, but not *noticeable* in the real world.

As students were spilling into the hallway after class and I was packing up my briefcase, Martina, fearing she had been disrespectful, approached my desk. "I'm sorry Professor Todd, I didn't mean to be rude. But last night I received an email from my grandmother in Venezuela."

Martina went on to reveal her family story to me: "My Nana told me how her parents had hoped for a better life for their children, one in which the daily fear of violence would be replaced by stability and security. Nana, even knowing how unsolvable and stubborn things are in my home country, clung to a vision for a better life for her children and grandchildren. But last night, Isabella, the little girl next door, a sweet five-year-old, was kidnapped, snatched through her bedroom window. As first light came to the barrio, word began to circulate among the neighbors that Izzy was being was held ransom so some guy could get drug debts paid."

Martina tearfully painted for me a sketch of the reality her family still faces: "Drugs, gangs, corrupt politicians, crooked cops, an unstable economy, the rarity of finding a good, well-paying job, fear-based living—those things are real. That God would intervene—would *rule* and *reign*? That is only something like Grandma's wishful prayer at Mass."

She could tell she had my compassionate attention, so she continued: "When I was young Nana taught me the Lord's Prayer. This morning as you were teaching, the line 'thy kingdom come, thy will be done,' it came back to me. I don't know how Nana, given the brutality of life that surrounds her, continues to pray that prayer. For me, I am uncertain of the whole thing—I can't pray it with any confidence, and I don't want to be a hypocrite. I feel stuck—like I am destined to live life with bitter disappointment, with dread that the bad things in life will never yield to the will of God. The skeptic in me cries out that the will of bad people being done is always going to be the norm."

Martina, slinging her backpack over her shoulder, let me off the hook of that awkward moment saying, "See you Wednesday, Professor." As she walked out the door, I sat down behind the teacher's desk. That was a lot to take in. I felt overwhelmed by the obviously true tension between what I enthusiastically taught and the lived reality of billions of people.

I walked to my car slowly that morning, my mind filled with the question: *What is the proper, honest, yet humble response that would honor Martina's story?*

## WHAT WOULD JESUS SAY TO MARTINA?

Martina's concern might stir similar issues in us: Why are fervent prayers not answered the way we want? Why is there so much suffering in the world? Why are evil deeds permitted by God? Those questions represent some of the primary ways we put God on trial. We want God to explain himself, to defend himself; we become like a district attorney and charge him with divine malpractice or heavenly negligence.

As I considered Martina's honest and passionate thoughts, at least one important reality came to mind, one that explains horrible scenes of child abduction and other forms of evil. *Up to this moment in history, life in the kingdom of God remains an invitation.* God does not normally force himself on people or arbitrarily influence every outcome in life. Rather, life in the kingdom as Jesus taught and modeled stands in the middle of human life as an opportunity. *Invitation* and *opportunity* create the opening for humans to decline the invitation and continue to do evil. This of course does not absolve God. We still wonder, *Why did God choose a way of interacting with human beings that allows for choice, for free will, when that opens the possibility of sin, of immorality that harms others?*

It is not the goal of this book to give a detailed explanation of the thorny problem of why a good and powerful God allows evil and suffering. Others have done that quite well.[1] Here I merely want to assert that God is purposeful and works on his own terms. God's chosen manner of revelation and the way he superintends history is from his great wisdom and is for our good. Even as Jesus proclaimed the gospel of the kingdom during his life, personal and social evil still occurred around him in every city he visited. Some suffering, within human bodies, he cured. Selected demons he drove out. Certain forms of civil evil he named, explained, resisted. But for the most part, life went on in approximately the way it had before Jesus exploded on the scene with his message about the inbreaking of God's kingdom.

Jesus never bullied or compelled actions against a person's will. Rather, he invited and encouraged:

*Come follow me,* by which Jesus meant align your life—the totality of your being, all your personal hopes and cultural, ethnic, and nationalistic dreams—with mine. Jesus was revealing that to live outside of, or misaligned to, what God is doing in and though him is the broad path that leads to multiplicities of destruction.

*The time is fulfilled,* which is to say that the long story of Israel was being fulfilled in and through Jesus and that "the kingdom of God is at hand." The rule and reign of God, God's expression of himself, is now closer to humanity than it has been since the first humans were banished from the Garden.

*Repent and believe* are in Jesus' mind the appropriate ways to respond to the fact that the time is fulfilled. Repenting (rethinking all of life) and believing (placing one's confidence in Jesus' announcement) are how one enters the kingdom, derives life from it, and becomes an ambassador of its inherent goodness.

*Seek first the kingdom of God* is Jesus' way of instructing us to make it the aim of our life that in all the places and spaces in which we live, what God wants done is in fact done. Look for, discern, be alert to the action of God in life and make it your priority—get involved with it. Seek to act and speak in harmony with what God is doing. This will mean dropping sinful willfulness and picking up a heart naturally bent toward and longing for obedience. There is a flow of God's kingdom working in the world today. Through relationship with Jesus, becoming his students in kingdom living, we learn to live, work, and play in union with that flow.

## THE KINGDOM OF GOD IN PARABLES

I was coming to see that Martina was not the only one straining to observe in real life that the kingdom of God is alive and well in the affairs of human beings. Jesus labored constantly, in word, deed, and manner of being, to explain and model life in the kingdom. He was consistently misunderstood.

At one point in his life (see Matthew 13), Jesus told a series of parables to help his hearers understand the complexities and subtleties of the inbreaking of God's kingdom. It is likely these parables are at the center of Matthew's strategy for presenting Jesus. These parables, which are teaching aids, are sources of insight for those struggling with religion, with God.

These parables are directed to the crowds; to all those who were following Jesus trying to figure out what he was teaching and what it meant and what to do about it. These parables were written for all of us who are honestly, but with various levels of spiritual sensitivity, trying to grapple with Jesus. In some people, the challenges of parables harden their hearts. Others are enlightened by their light, and the parables produce confidence to follow Jesus.[2]

A core concern for many de-churched people is this: If, as Jesus says, the kingdom is already present, then why aren't things fixed? The parables of Jesus help us in this regard because they often have to do with waiting, with patience, and with the disappointment and confusion that comes with anticipating and expecting things to turn out right.

The slow, steady growth of the kingdom over millennia seems wrong. The unhurried nature of God makes him look out of touch or heartless. It allows for too much sin, evil, and suffering. Should God be seen as complicit and therefore chastised? *Silence is violence. Slowness enables oppression—it is the privilege of those in power.* Do we all need to command God? *Enough is enough! Get up. Stand up. Speak up. Do something!*

A moment of honesty is needed here: things are not just bad in our cities, government, and schools. They are bad in our hearts and our corresponding behaviors. We want God to judge and stop the evil that appears in the news, but we are protective of our own thoughts, words, and deeds, and don't with the same urgency ask God to intervene in our hearts. To pursue thinking about God and religion with righteousness, this inconsistency is something we must reflect on and change.

A parable seeks to give understanding by using a common point of reference to explain something new. All of Jesus' hearers would have understood sowing seeds, grain and weeds, yeast and dough. From these simple things of life, Jesus reveals the magnificence of God's kingdom.

*The Parable of the Sower* (Matthew 13:1-8; 18-23) alerts us to the fact that, while in Christ God sows the good seed of the kingdom, not all the ground on which the seed falls is equally receptive. The seed is said to be sown *in the heart*. A lack of receptivity in the human heart is a significant answer to the dilemma of ongoing suffering. When our hearts are not receptive, *the evil one snatches away what was sown.* We want to blame God for his kingdom not coming with perfection. Jesus observes responsibility in other things: the evil one, those who quickly fall away when trouble comes, the worries of this life, the deceitfulness of wealth, seeking pleasure more than the kingdom—these are the things that choke life from the seed of the kingdom.

This parable asks us as individuals to notice what kind of soil we are and how we hear Jesus' message of the kingdom.[3] It describes the interaction between what God is doing to sow his goodness among humanity and our response to it. God is good and generously, lavishly, spreads the seed of the kingdom. But rival kingdoms of the spiritual and earthly sort remain active, doing their harmful work. Furthermore, issues of the human heart—inconsistent, unthoughtful commitment to the kingdom—frustrate the work of God.

Together these realities yield the world Martina rightly laments.

*The Parable of the Wheat and Weeds* (Matthew 13:24-30, 36-43) further reveals that an enemy of God is at work in the world sowing *weeds* among God's *wheat*. In this parable God is directly challenged: "I thought you were sowing healthy wheat—what is the deal with these weeds growing among the wheat?" Further, people wondered, "To work alongside you, shouldn't we go pull the weeds now before they ruin the whole crop?" "No," Jesus replies, "wheat and weeds will grow together until the final harvest."

The kingdom of God is quietly present in the world while not yet wiping out all opposition to it.[4] Our frustration with evil will not go away until God finally has the last say at the final judgment, at the moment he finally insists on justice—in our heart and in the world—and renews heaven and earth.

*The Parable of the Mustard Seed* (Matthew 13:31-32) shows that the kingdom will have a small, even tiny beginning but will be ever growing and will come to a large and glorious fulfillment. Through this parable we learn that the kingdom does not impose itself on anyone. The kingdom of God is like the smallest, the humblest of all seeds known to Jesus' hearers. Although it is largely imperceptible, first under the ground, out of sight, that seed grows a tap root and root system. Next, it emerges as a small shoot above the soil. Continuing to grow, the mustard seed finally becomes the largest of garden plants and "becomes a tree, so that the birds come and make nests in its branches" (v. 32). The kingdom of God provides a source of life, a system of life (branches, twigs, and leaves) so that we can perch our lives in it.

***The Parable of the Yeast*** (Matthew 13:33) tells us that, in the same way yeast spreads through a whole lump of dough, the kingdom will someday permeate and transform all human life. This leavening process is not visible to our eyes. But it is happening. It is real.

By the way, none of what I have just said about the parables of the kingdom is an excuse for not working diligently against issues of injustice. The Bible is full of instructions that implore God's people to seek justice. The ideas being explored here simply set the context for the work of justice every follower of Jesus is expected to engage with.

Thinking again of my conversation with Martina, I realized that what Jesus was teaching is true of our world. Most of the time we cannot see God at work. He chooses to be hidden. But God is real. He is at work in our real lives. Life is going on as normal, but the kingdom is within our grasp. This implies, as is seen in the next two parables, that a decision is called for to believe in, trust in, and follow Jesus.[5] Tom Wright gets to the core of the matter:

> God's sovereign plan to put the world to rights is waiting for [us] to sign on.
>
> That is the force of what Jesus is saying . . . and it holds out an invitation, to this day, to those who are anxious about the future: God's sovereign rule of the world, his healing love, are not only yours for the grasping, but are waiting for your help.[6]

Someday, God's reality will be revealed, and the worship depicted at the end of the story, celebrating the full flowering of the kingdom will be real too:

Hallelujah!
Salvation and glory and power belong to our God,
    for true and just are his judgments. . . .
Hallelujah!
    For our Lord God Almighty reigns.
Let us rejoice and be glad
    and give him glory! (Revelation 19:1-7)

*The Parable of the Hidden Treasure* invites us to look within, to become conscious of our deep desires, of that on which we place supreme value. Namely, once we hear Jesus' gospel of the kingdom, are we willing to sell or exchange all that we must to enter the kingdom of God, to live—as Jesus did—with God's kingdom as our highest priority? As we repent and enter the kingdom of God "all the heart's quests are revalued";[7] we experience a "detachment for the sake of [a new] attachment."[8] The words of James K. A. Smith are memorable to me: "you are what you love, . . . and you might not love what you think" you do.[9] Following Jesus in the kingdom of God creates new, rightly ordered loves and habituates them in our daily life.

Jesus once asked a man a question that is spiritually universal: "What do you want?" (John 1:38). Determining what we truly treasure is a basic building block for following Jesus. Smith goes on to say, "Jesus' command to follow him is a command to align our loves and longings with his—to want what God wants, to desire what God desires, to hunger and thirst after God and crave a world where he is all in all—a vision encapsulated by the shorthand 'kingdom of God.'"[10]

Jesus' parables about the treasure are meant to function as an "imagination station"[11] that "incubates our loves and longings . . . that index[es] our hearts toward God and his kingdom."[12] This is crucial because "to be conformed to the image of Jesus is not only to think God's thoughts after him, but to desire what God desires—and that requires the recalibration of our heart habits and the recapturing of our imaginations."[13]

**The Parable of the Pearl of Great Price** works very much like the parable of the treasure. It helps us determine that which is most important in our lives, that which we most passionately seek. It helps us wonder, *Am I seeking the kingdom the way the pearl merchant seeks fine pearls?* As Jesus commanded in Matthew 6:33, *Am I seeking first the kingdom of God? If I found the best pearl available (the kingdom) would I sell all my lesser pearls and leverage all other assets to get it?* Smith reveals the crucial point of the parables of the treasure and the pearl: "Jesus is a teacher who doesn't just inform our intellect but forms our very loves. He isn't content to simply deposit new ideas into your mind; he is after nothing less than your wants, your loves, your longings."[14]

For our work here, thinking of burned-out Christians and church leaders, we should note the role of disordered human desire as a prime source of suffering and evil. Our own disordered desires release pain in the world. God in his love and wisdom makes space for this sort of human agency. This is turn makes God vulnerable to the criticism of *why is the world the way it is?* Setting aside natural disasters, the most honest answer is that the world is full of pain, injustice, inequality, and suffering because of human choices, choices rooted in disordered desires.

Such choices are what makes life a vanity and a chasing after the wind (see Ecclesiastes 1:14; 2:11, 17). Or, to paraphrase Jesus, drink of lesser things than the kingdom and you will thirst again . . . but whoever drinks the water of the gospel of the kingdom will never thirst. Indeed, the water in my gospel will become in them a spring of water welling up to eternal life (see John 4:13-14).

**The Parable of the Net** depicts the moment when fishermen of Jesus' day brought their net up out of the water. Some of the fish in the net had a reputation for looking appetizing and tasting good and therefore would be easy to sell. Some of the fish, however, were judged as low quality, and would have been thrown back into the sea. Like the parable of the wheat and weeds, this parable tells us that though God is casting his net as deep and wide as possible, seeking to "catch" everyone, a day is coming when the wicked will be separated from the righteous. God will do this motivated by his clear, all-knowing judgment. This judgment is motivated by his just insistence that his whole creation be renewed. Such renewal will not be able to tolerate those who have not made God and his kingdom their greatest love and highest priority.

Parables were not just nice sayings. They were a subtle form of an invitation to enter the kingdom that Jesus said was available through becoming his disciple. Probing the depths of our desires, the inward, hidden reality from which we make the decisions of life, Jesus said:

Whoever *wants* to be my disciple must deny themselves and take up their cross daily and follow me. For whoever *wants* to save their life will lose it, but whoever loses their life for me will save it. What good is it for someone to gain the whole world, and yet lose or forfeit their very self? Whoever is ashamed of me and my words, the Son of Man will be ashamed of them when he comes in his glory and in the glory of the Father and of the holy angels. (Luke 9:23-26, emphasis added)

## GOOD CHURCH . . . GOOD RELIGION

"If he says the word *kingdom* one more time, I am going to go crazy!"

Elbowing him in the ribs, that is what I whispered to my buddy sometime in 1978 during a typical sermon by John Wimber, the founder of the worldwide movement of Vineyard churches. Wimber was captivated by the depiction of Jesus in the Gospels. He wanted to take Jesus seriously, which he knew meant giving close attention to Jesus' teaching on the kingdom of God.

Seeking to be ambassadors of the kingdom has, over the last four-plus decades, led the Vineyard to bring the kingdom to bear on human brokenness by being agents of healing to many thousands of people. Thousands of others have been delivered from drugs, alcohol, and sexual addictions. Hundreds of thousands of undernourished families have been provided meals. Block parties in impoverished neighborhoods brought joy and racial reconciliation. Rundown homes of the elderly and poor were repaired. The mentally ill were loved and shepherded to appropriate care. The homeless were given shelter. Immigrants were valued for their essential humanity and set on a path to full inclusion.

In Vineyard churches, like thousands of churches in every denomination, the kingdom of God was doing, as the parables above suggest, its slow, steady, but meaningful work. Was evil still rampant in impoverished neighborhoods simultaneous to this godly work? Yes. But that fact does not indict God. It sets a choice before us. James nails it: "What causes fights and quarrels among you? Don't they come from your desires that battle within you? You desire but do not have, so you kill. You covet but you cannot get what you want, so you quarrel and fight" (James 4:1-2).

In so doing we perpetuate pain, suffering, and evil—we become part of a rival kingdom.

## ENTER, SEEK, AND RECEIVE

How are followers of Jesus meant to respond to Jesus' words and works concerning the kingdom of God? We are meant to hear an invitation and give a positive RSVP to enter, seek, and receive.

We enter by placing our confidence in Jesus and beginning to follow him, giving ourselves to him as his students, his apprentices in kingdom living. For God's kingdom is where Jesus lives and moves and has his being. We seek because we have come to think highly of Jesus. We have taken to heart, truly, the greatness, love, and power of God in and through Jesus. Coming to trust him, we seek him, his kingdom, and his righteousness. We receive the kingdom—the expressed present action of God—as we give ourselves to it, like a child.

The kingdom of God is not like a sophisticated lock to be picked or a theological riddle to be solved only by spiritual masterminds. In contrast, reception of the kingdom, according to Jesus, is best facilitated by childlike qualities: innocence, humility, and dependence. Finding those virtues requires dropping our guardedness. It means stopping the self-bluff that we are in control. It requires coming to know that our brokenness, transformed in and by God's kingdom, can be made beautiful and useful.

## HOPE

Last night I watched a television documentary about a team of people who search for underwater plane crashes, trying to solve the mysteries surrounding the plane itself, the purpose of the flight, and why it crashed. Divers use lights and cameras to illumine and capture images of the crash site on the ocean floor. Initially, the pictures look like pieces of trash with barnacles attached. Over time, putting the pieces visually back together, these experts can determine the type and owner of the plane and some details about what caused the crash.

We all have experienced some aspect of a spiritual crash. The *good* does indeed seem trashed and spread wide on the floor of human life. We wonder how to be present as agents of good with faith and hope.

Here's how we do this: we can stand in our moment of history. We can work here. Let's you and I be like the search team. Let's *see what this is*—this world in which we are invited to follow Jesus. Piecing original parts back together, using the aims of Jesus as our guiding idea, let's make meaning of what we find. Let see what the world was always meant to be, even if it seems mucked up and partially buried by the realities of shifting patterns of sin and the growing barnacles of evil.

In the chapters to come we strive to see Jesus faithfully and fruitfully through understanding his aims, in his own words, from his own mind, through his own heart. Seeing Jesus, meeting him on his terms, is central to everything Christian. As described in these words attributed to Tom Wright,

If you want to know who God is, look at Jesus.

If you want to know what it means to be human, look at Jesus.

If you want to know what love is, look at Jesus.

If you want to know what grief is, look at Jesus.

And go on looking until you're not just a spectator,

but you're actually part of the drama which has him as the central character.

The biblical book of Hebrews was written to encourage struggling Christians. Its goal, in the face of religious confusion and disheartening conflict, was to help those stuck in quagmires of faith to stick with it. As Eugene Peterson wrote in his introduction to Hebrews in *The Message*, "Religion can very well get in the way of what God is doing for us . . . and the antidote for this bad religion is God's action revealed in Jesus, period."[15] Therefore, the writer of Hebrews, giving those hurt by the church a glimmer of hope, says, "We must never stop looking to Jesus. He is the leader of our faith, and he is the one who makes our faith complete. . . . Think about him so that you won't get discouraged and stop trying" (Hebrews 12:2-3 ERV).

## EXERCISE
### APPLYING THE AIMS OF JESUS TO MY LIFE

1. How do you hold the tension of the nature of the kingdom of God, which is already present but not yet fulfilled? What are some areas where you have seen the kingdom come to bear in tangible ways in your own life and the lives of others? On what issue does your heart still cry out, *How long, O Lord? Will you hide your face forever?* This is an authentic invitation to lament *with* Jesus as slowly as necessary. And it's beautiful. It puts you in his loving and gracious presence as you ask for any amendment of life that he shows you.

2. Has harm from the church or misplaced blame on God slowed or blocked your previous passion to seek justice and do good in the church and the world? If yes, looking back, what issue or situation first broke your heart so much that you had to do something? What joyful vision did you once have of things being different? Sit with those positive ideas. Let them wash over you afresh. Notice what new or returning ideas arise. Is there a momentum into which you feel invited to lean?

---

You might begin with this prayer:

*Lord, I am frustrated. I have tried to be good and do good. But evil seems immovable, and I am bruised by the experience of pain I endured in the church. I invite your healing. Please refresh my vision. Stir up my gifts and restore to me the joy of my salvation. Revive my calling to follow you and to be an ambassador of your kingdom.*

What words of your own would you like to add?

# 6

# WHAT ABOUT ALL THE BAD THINGS DONE IN GOD'S NAME?

## JESUS TAUGHT THAT ETERNAL LIFE EMPOWERS GOOD RELIGION

*This is eternal life: that they know you, the only true*
*God, and Jesus Christ, whom you have sent.*

**JOHN 17:3**

*Very truly I tell you, whoever hears my word and believes*
*him who sent me has eternal life and will not be*
*judged but has crossed over from death to life.*

**JOHN 5:24**

*I am the resurrection and the life. The one who believes in me will live,*
*even though they die; and whoever lives by believing in me will never die.*

**JOHN 11:25-26**

**I am a sincere Christian.** I do dumb things. I do not have the capacity to be right about every topic. I commit sins. Sometimes those things hurt others. What is true for me is normative for all Christians. Reasonable people forgive a lack of perfection.

But sometimes we Christians, in God's name, get things badly, damagingly wrong. And people know it. It raises honest questions about whether the church is truly good, or just a place where imperfect people act righteous while doing and saying things that harm others.

This is one reason appealing to the "universe" or to the "spiritual aspect of life" is so common. That way there is no group of people—like a church—to assess and condemn. It is private, so there is little or no tension with social or religious norms. The universe speaking cannot be tested, while claiming the Bible is speaking is a consistent invitation to an argument.

I don't blame people for taking cover in the universe. They are trying to find a way to relate to something bigger than themselves without having to do so in and through the church, a place where they have experienced people doing bad things in the name of God.

Robert is just that sort of person. I don't know him well, but I bump into him occasionally at the gym. As I observed his various interactions over a period of months, he seemed to me a thoughtful and kind person.

Early one morning I came to see that he was deeply empathetic as well. Our lockers happened to be near each other and after showering, we were dressing for work while exchanging pleasantries. Walking out the front door, before coming to the asphalt parking lot, Robert stopped and asked, "How is it that Christians can be so mean, even be racist?"

"Why is that question on your mind this morning?"

"My neighbor, he is white supremacist, an out-and-out racist; he even claims the title with exuberant joy. He wears his intentional racist views like a badge proclaiming his truth. And then, unbelievably to me, he goes to church every week with his family. He speaks horribly about immigrants, wishing that they would just go back to their home countries. He shows no concern for those trapped in physical illness, emotional pain, or economic hardship. To him they are just a pain in the rear. He says he wishes they would stop complaining, stop being a drain on society, and just slink away out of sight."

"I'm so sorry that is your experience . . ."

Before I could say more, Robert interjected, "I snoop around in religious things when they pop up in life or in the news. I have some interest in spirituality—I mean surely there is a god. But I can't get past my neighbor and others like him. Hate and Jesus don't go together in my moral imagination. I don't want to get mixed up with that kind of people. I am left wondering, Is my neighbor an outlier or is he a common product of the church? Truthfully, I am a bit frightened to find out."

Someday God's perfections will emerge and will heal all human pain, suffering, angst. God will sort out those who claim to follow him and those who do follow him, and he will fix me. I long for the day. But for now, for Robert and me, and probably for you, we are left with disturbing questions about all the bad things done in God's name.

## THE GOODNESS OF JUDGMENT

When some people judge, their harsh angry rejection is enough to make us run for the hills, cancel those people, or cower in fear. No one likes the incensed shouting of ignorant, unkind, uncaring people. But when certain special people judge, when they make discriminating decisions, we place high value on them. For instance, when a medical technician interprets an important test result, we trust them and value their ability to judge between a cancer cell, a precancerous cell, and a normal cell. We trust dentists to judge our teeth and gums. We trust baseball umpires to judge pitches and to clearly name them balls or strikes.

Jesus said of himself, "For the Son of Man is going to come in his Father's glory with his angels, and then he will reward each person according to what they have done" (Matthew 16:27). Concerning judgment, Jesus employed simple images like light and darkness, sheep and goats, and wheat and tares. These descriptions illustrated that someday there will be a separation of people: those who love God and his ways and who pursue them and align their lives to them, in contrast to those who don't care about God or his agenda, who want nothing to do with him, who would not enjoy his presence. Each will be recognized for who they are and dealt with accordingly. Those who can't stand God and want nothing to do with him will have their place. Jesus called this place hell.

This is not a bad attitude on God's part. Nor is it judgmentalism. It is simply naming what is real: a cavity or not, a strike or a ball, a wonderfully differentiated liver cell versus a poorly differentiated cancer cell. What would we think of a God who did not understand good and evil, who could not see the difference between the two? Would you love and respect such a God? Would you follow Jesus if God was morally blind?

God's judgment is not rooted in him impatiently losing his temper like a fed-up parent. It springs from his loving purposes. God's *judgment* brings his *justice*. It is his insistence that creation come to be what he meant it to be. Surely this would exclude theft, war, rape, racism, unjust poverty, dishonesty, and various other evils and injustices. But some people, even knowing it is wrong, persist in those behaviors, marring God's creation. On judgment day God will say, "Stop it! That's enough! No more! No more harming *my* creation, *my* humanity." It will be like a referee noticing that the game clock has hit 0.00—game over. Time's up! Let the final separation begin.

I wonder if you caught the italicized *my* above. It is crucial. We think we own ourselves. We talk about my neighborhood, my city, my country, etc. Of course, that is fine on one level, but on another level, we forget that humanity is designed by God for his purposes, his undertaking, not ours. His preservation of humanity though his justice-bringing nature and ultimate judgment is a demonstration that we exist for his loving, wise purposes. Those who insist on fighting that reality, those who are weeds, darkness, and goats, will someday be granted their wishes to have nothing to do with him. To some degree, God's judgment of us is simply his recognition of our judgment of him.

How we imagine God judging is a key indicator of our connection to religion, to church. For those with church hurts, they often have an experience of God's judgment based on being treated in destructive, condemnatory ways in the name of God.

Tom Wright helps us see that God's judgment should be welcomed, cherished even:

All future judgment is highlighted basically as good news, not bad. Why so? It is good news, first, because the one through whom God's justice will finally sweep the world is not a hard-hearted, arrogant, or vengeful tyrant but rather the Man of Sorrows, who was acquainted with grief; the Jesus who loved sinners and died for them; the Messiah who took the world's judgment upon himself on the cross.[1]

How we interact with God's judgment, his persistence in seeing that his is will done, makes a difference. Again, Wright is illuminating:

When human beings give their heartfelt allegiance to and worship that which is not God, they progressively cease to reflect the image of God. One of the primary laws of human life is that you become like what you worship; what's more, you reflect what you worship not only to the object itself but also outward to the world around. Those who worship money increasingly define themselves in terms of it and increasingly treat other people as creditors, debtors, partners, or customers rather than as human beings. Those who worship sex define themselves in terms of it (their preferences, their practices, their past histories) and increasingly treat other people as actual or potential sex objects. Those who worship power define themselves in terms of it and treat other people as either collaborators, competitors, or pawns. These and many other forms of idolatry combine in a thousand ways, all of them damaging to the image-bearing quality of the people concerned and of those whose lives they touch.[2]

But we do not have to be stuck there. At all times there stands before humanity an opportunity to make the decision to trust and follow Jesus, to invite his life to define and direct our life to the end that we become agents of good religion, conveying the goodness of the world to come now in our world.

Recently at church I was moved by this closing prayer for our time of worship:

> Almighty God, who has created humankind in your own image; grant us grace fearlessly to contend against evils, and to make no peace with oppression; and, that we may reverently use our freedom, help us to employ it in the maintenance of justice among men and nations, to the glory of your holy name; through Jesus Christ our Lord.[3]

Prayers like that are practices that rehabituate one's heart toward alignment with God and his purposes in and through humanity. Over time they move a soul from dark to light, from weed to wheat, from goat to sheep. God is not dumb or blind. He notices what is real about us and calls it out. Knowledge of eternity is meant to shape the present.

## ETERNAL LIFE EMPOWERS GOOD RELIGION

To think clearly about eternal life, let's first pin down a definition of *eternity*. The word refers to unbounded timelessness that is suitably used of God's existence,[4] and that which includes time but also transcends it. The things of human life happen within human history and are superintended by God who works in our space/realm/time while existing on an eternal plane all his own.

It is that eternity—with its Trinity of persons, its perfections, and its joys—that is being brought to bear on earth in and through the person and work of Jesus.

Jesus knew that the addition of a little religion to one's life was not what his Father had in view for broken sinners who were misaligned to his purposes. In Matthew, Mark, and Luke, Jesus called people to *life in the kingdom* as the new path toward humanity as God intended, as the antidote for bad religion. In John's Gospel Jesus is quoted using a different phrase to connote the same full-life transformation, *eternal life.*

- "For God so loved the world that he gave his one and only Son, that whoever believes in him shall not perish but have eternal life." (John 3:16)
- "Whoever believes in the Son has eternal life." (John 3:36)
- "Very truly I tell you, whoever hears my word and believes him who sent me has eternal life and will not be judged but has crossed over from death to life." (John 5:24)
- "My sheep listen to my voice; I know them, and they follow me. I give them eternal life, and they shall never perish; no one will snatch them out of my hand." (John 10:27-28)
- "Anyone who loves their life will lose it, while anyone who hates their life in this world will keep it for eternal life." (John 12:25)
- "Now this is eternal life: that they know you, the only true God, and Jesus Christ, whom you have sent." (John 17:3)

But what is the reality to which the words *eternal life* point? Put differently, what does eternity have to do with today?

We can get at this by looking again at John 17:3. First, let's observe what eternal life is not. It is not merely something that one receives at the moment of death. It is not simply more life or never-ceasing life. Nor is it life that is confined to a certain place or sphere, such as heaven.

Eternal life is a description of "a present and future rela-tionship with God based on the redemptive work of the Son."[5] One scholar further describes it saying that "those who know God in the present have an incorruptible fellowship with God that cannot be severed or impugned by death."[6]

Scholars think that for John *eternal life* was his way of high-lighting "the inner experience of salvation, of life in the kingdom of God" and that *kingdom of God* and *eternal life* are virtual equiv-alents, both signifying "the state of blessedness that one partici-pates in through faith in Jesus." This state of blessedness comes from "the life of the age to come, the very life that God has, God's own kind of life, divine life."[7] Thus, "Whoever has the Son has [this] life" (1 John 5:12). This life is of course mysterious, but not that only. It is seen, known, and experienced: "We know that we have passed from death to life, because we love each other. Anyone who does not love remains in death" (1 John 3:14).

Eternal life is a *kind* of life. It has a quality to it that is obvious. It cannot be hidden. The city lights of Denver, Colorado, cannot be concealed during a cloudless night flight. They command the attention of anyone in a window seat. Eternal life in a human life is similarly observable. As Jesus put it, "a town built on a hill cannot be hidden" (Matthew 5:14).

Primarily, eternal life has to do with experiential, firsthand knowledge of God and his Son Jesus, whom he sent to earth. This rich interactive knowledge produces in us a different *quality* of living. A focus on quality, on receiving a different sort of life, a life immersed in the fragrances and perfections of eternity, is the source of a good life, a servant life, a liberating-others life, a life that models God's intentions and spreads the scent of good religion.

Dallas Willard's translation of John 3:16 illuminates our work here: "God's care for humanity was so great that he sent his unique Son among us, so that those who count on him might not lead a futile and failing existence, but have the undying life of God himself."[8]

Eternal life starts now, in this life, as soon as one has the life of Christ alive in them. Yes, this life will never end. As Jesus said, "I am the resurrection and the life. The one who believes in me will live, even though they die" (John 11:25). Jesus' words are a statement of truth with an invitation attached. They help us see that to try to create and possess one's own life, to pursue it selfishly and hold on to it greedily, does not lead to being an ambassador of Jesus, to good religion. Only Jesus' quality of life in and through us can do that.

## RECEIVING ETERNAL LIFE

John's stated purpose for telling the Jesus story is that his readers would come to believe in Jesus and thereby have an eternal kind of life. For instance,

- These [things Jesus did] are written that you may believe that Jesus is the Messiah, the Son of God, and that by believing you may have life in his name. (John 20:31)
- I write these things to you who believe in the name of the Son of God so that you may know that you have eternal life. (1 John 5:13)

Through talk of eternal life, John was not seeking to produce people who would someday become disembodied souls floating around heaven forever without any connection to God's first creation, God's story, and God's eternal purposes for his reembodied friends. The word *reembodied* signifies that in the new heaven and new earth followers of Jesus will have new bodies suitable to that new reality and appropriate for God's purposes in and through such bodies.

What John seeks to communicate is that life in the age to come, with its hopes, joys, and perfection, has come forward into the present through Jesus, and that in knowing him we can have that life now. When this life is placed before us there is a decision to be made. John said of Jesus, "He came to that which was his own, but his own did not receive him" (John 1:11).

Eternal life is not imposed on anyone. It must be desired as a core aspect of becoming a follower of Jesus, of receiving him, his kingdom life, his orientation toward the Father. To do this some of us will have to shift our gaze for a period: from deconstruction based in church hurts to constructing renewed faith around the person and work of Jesus, of the eternal God-Life he brought to earth and continues to offer.

For those who follow Jesus comprehensively, eternal life creates a lifestyle. Habits, conduct, language, dress, responses to others, and interpersonal relationships are all made new by having Jesus, and his kind of life, at the center of our life.

Eternal life is the fuller story of standard human life. Sometimes the good religion of that fuller life breaks out in full view.

## ETERNAL LIFE IS THE FULLER STORY

The Reverend Hewitt Sawyers, a seventy-three-year-old Black man, has been pastor at Primitive Baptist Church for many decades. His face says love and his countenance says welcome while his graying beard conveys the wisdom he is known for around town. He is the kind of man who makes me think, *Do I call him Mr., Reverend, or Sir?* I wanted to use the word that conveyed the most respect. Speaking at a pastor's lunch in the Nashville area, there came a moment when you could hear a pin drop on the carpet as Pastor Sawyers recounted the fuller story being told in Franklin, Tennessee.

Franklin has consistently been named "best small town" in America. However, that is not the whole story. Even though Sawyers grew up mere steps from downtown Franklin, he avoided the public square because of the Confederate monument known locally as "Chip." Sawyers lived through the Jim Crow era and the public square wasn't a place where Black people felt welcome. The town square, surrounded by iconic tree-lined streets, framed by sidewalks yielding entrances to boutique shops and charming southern restaurants, has become a popular destination for Civil War buffs and shoppers looking for quaint bargains. I work just off the square, so I can tell you the vast majority of visitors to downtown and the Civil War sites are white.

The Black population, who still don't tend to hang out downtown, see a fuller story. They know the history and feel the dark past in their bones. For over fifty years slaves were sold there—some who were great-great-grandparents to the local living Black population. But because of Reverend Sawyers and the leadership of a few others, things began to change.

This is the story.

Following the tragedies of the 2017 rally in Charlottesville, Virginia, "Franklin area pastors and community leaders of all races gathered for a prayer vigil around Franklin's public square. . . . From that gathering, discussions began . . . about how all aspects of Franklin's history were not adequately acknowledged in the downtown square." Nothing described or proclaimed the brutality "faced by enslaved Black people through the years in that same public square."[9]

Instead of tearing the statue down, a few local pastors, among whom Reverend Sawyers was a key influencer, as well as a group of community leaders raised support and funds to erect five historical markers in the public square. "The five markers tell the story of an old courthouse on the square where slaves were bought and sold, the Battle of Franklin, the US Colored Troops Soldiers, the 1867 race riot that occurred in Franklin and Reconstruction."[10] It is deeply sobering to read the description of the "market house that stood on the square in the early years of Franklin's founding and was used for the purchasing and selling of human beings."[11]

A statue honoring the US Colored Troops was erected in front of the Courthouse, which had assisted in the buying and selling of slaves. Joe Frank Howard, the sculptor, told a local newspaper that he was proud to create the statue of a heroic Black soldier, working to free his people, "people that were not classified as human beings. They were cattle or some type of work animals."[12]

I've stood in front of the statue trying to take in the genius of it. I'm sure I've got more to do in that regard, but I notice one important thing emanating from it: Black people, like all God's human creation have a deep and essential dignity within them, a grandeur that commands love and respect. God has "put eternity in their hearts" (Ecclesiastes 3:11 NKJV). Alongside the cruelty and sorrow of slavery and modern racism, there is a longing for the fuller story of what is real about Black people and their Creator: they have full image-bearing worth and a full place of welcome in the story of humanity.

## THE DAY OF THE LORD

Things are not perfect in Franklin. There was pushback against the markers and the statue. A local chapter of the United Daughters of the Confederacy argued in court to stop the process.[13] The Confederate statue and the new markers are all a reminder of the brutalities of which humankind is capable. But at least there is now the fuller story.

Feeling empathy for those struggling with religion and church, I thought of this story as I was thinking through the earlier parts of this chapter. We can't say that the church is good and pretend that bad things are not done in the name of Christianity, of God. The actions of church history standing tall in the squares of history say otherwise. We must recognize that church-based suffering of all kinds is real. That is a true story.

But there is a fuller story that is also real, one that will be revealed on "the day of the Lord," the day when God sorts things out and remakes this brutal world into a beautiful one. On that day the statues of evil, pain, and injustice will come down, never again to have the power to retraumatize people. The new markers that God will put up will proclaim, testify to, and insist on his justice, his righteousness, his perfections.

The apostle John, whose words we have used throughout this chapter, received the revelation of the fuller story:

> Then I saw "a new heaven and a new earth," for the first heaven and the first earth had passed away. . . . I saw the Holy City, the new Jerusalem, coming down out of heaven from God, prepared as a bride beautifully dressed for her husband. And I heard a loud voice from the throne saying, "Look! God's dwelling place is now among the people, and he will dwell with them. They will be his people, and God himself will be with them and be their God. 'He will wipe every tear from their eyes. There will be no more death' or mourning or crying or pain, for the old order of things has passed away."
>
> He who was seated on the throne said, "I am making everything new!" Then he said, "Write this down, for these words are trustworthy and true." (Revelation 21:1-5)

They were on a scroll, not in a town square, but John nevertheless set up new markers containing the revelation of God's fuller story. Everyone is welcome to walk up to them, to read them, to take them to life-altering heart. Everyone is invited to make their words the story of their life. They are words that give hope for the healing of bad religion. They animate good religion.

---
### EXERCISE
## APPLYING THE AIMS OF JESUS TO MY LIFE

1. It may feel buried under disappointment and discontentment, but in what ways do you still sense motivation to join with God in the redemption of the world?

2. What specific social injustice, mission, evangelism, or ministry to the church is connected to that motive? What are the practical ways in which you feel called to be creative or to lead?

3. Holding those things prayerfully before God, do you sense a calling to take that step in faith?

---

You might begin with this prayer:

*Lord, you know how hard I worked to prepare for a ministry of loving and serving your people in the church. You saw my desire to be a positive person, to be an agent of healing, to work against injustice in the world. I also know you see my broken heart, crumpled will, and discouraged soul. I feel like my sincere passionate efforts have done little good. My labors have been crushed under the weight of being judged and misunderstood. I feel used by leadership and then cast aside when I no longer fit political realities, a new season, or a new vision. I ask to see a fresh glimpse of eternity, a vision of your fulfilled purposes. I ask you to stir up eternity in my heart. I ask for that fuller story to invade my present story.*

What words of your own would you like to add?

# 7

# CAN I TRUST THE CHURCH TO BE AN INSTRUMENT OF RESTORATION?

## JESUS WAS A HEALER

*[Jesus] was moved with compassion for them, because they were weary and scattered, like sheep having no shepherd.*

**MATTHEW 9:36 ESV**

*I am willing; be cleansed.*

**LUKE 5:13 NASB**

*Where two or three gather in my name, there am I with them.*

**MATTHEW 18:20**

**Whether at Sunday worship** or at a fellowship event of some sort, Sally and Carter were always neatly dressed in traditional Midwest attire. They made practical comfort look effortless. Although they were not pretentious, something about the way they carried themselves seemed buttoned-up or pulled together. Over the years I knew them to have delightful affection for one another. The affection they each possessed easily overflowed through an uncommon ability to be hospitable and keenly present to others. People consistently praised them as a wonderful couple. Their essential kindness made them the sort of people with whom one can disclose the challenges of life.

Sally and Carter have been married for twenty-seven years and are almost empty nesters. A son in his senior year of high school remains. Much of their church disappointment and pain come from watching their children wander from the faith. Starting at about thirteen years old, each of Sally and Carter's three children began to have religious and churchly doubts. This added to and complicated Carter and Sally's own nonverbalized church hurts and the worries that were secretly troubling them.

Sally and Carter attended one of my small group conversations focused on naming and describing the spiritual angst of those struggling with church.

When it was their turn to speak, Sally took out a piece of paper and Carter swiped to the notes app on his phone—each now ready with their thoughtfully prepared remarks. They got my attention.

Sally began, "We have standards in our family for human sexuality, but we are not mean about it. In fact, we are very conscious of being tolerant, of showing love to others. Nevertheless, because we have a standard, some people assume we hate them and are against them. We don't know how to show the love of Jesus without compromising what we hold to be the truth."

Carter spoke up, "We have a grandson, age four, who is beginning to show feminine traits. What does it mean to fulfill our Christian obligations to him, our daughter, and our son-in-law?"

Sally interjected, "Unmet expectations related to answered prayer are causing trust issues for us. Throughout the teenage years of our children, we prayed to God for their protection, asking that they would stay close to Jesus. Our prayers were not answered. We are wounded by this. It is confusing. In truth, these unanswered prayers have caused doubt to enter our hearts. Does God not hear us? Are our prayers hindered by some hidden sin? Does God not care? Or, in some way concealed to us, is God working in the lives of our children?"

Carter spoke last, saying, "We just know that when we are given space to think about it, as we are in groups like this, we are significantly hurting and confused about the central role church has played in our lives—both great good and disturbing pain. Our spiritual life is bewildering. We feel like our faith is being constantly tested. The worst part is that when we have dared to tell others in church what is happening and how we are feeling about it, all we get in return are tired and stale pat answers with a tinge of shaming us for not being better parents, better Christians."

Life hurts. Tragically, spiritual malpractice rubs the sore, increasing the pain. Bad religion is not just wrong thinking isolated in an individual. Its effect is more like the multicar pileups that occur in foggy, mountainous driving conditions. The fog of bad religion causes heartache and suffering to reverberate in every direction. The throbbing in one's soul is life altering.

## BAD RELIGION: IT'S AGAINST JESUS' RELIGION

In his ministry Jesus named and described some of the most common aspects of bad religion and spiritual confusion. Found in the Gospels (see Matthew 23:13-32; Mark 12:38-40; Luke 11:37-52), these statements of Jesus are often referred to as woes spoken to religious leaders. To get a feel for the word *woe*, imagine Jesus using the word to convey something like this: "How misfortunate are the religious leaders that they don't get what is really going on. This is a grief for them, and it causes grief for others. Missing the point like they do is ruinous trouble. It is a calamity that afflicts them and their hearers. Because of their bad religion, misery spreads to all elements of spiritual life."

*The Message* version of the Bible calls these supposed spiritual guides hopeless frauds, who are "full of arrogant stupidity" (see Matthew 23 MSG)! Tom Wright calls these sections of Scripture the "condemnation of the Scribes and Pharisees."[1] The New Living Translation laments the sorrow that awaits them.

Would it help you to know that Jesus detests bad religion more than you?

And yet, no matter how repulsed we are by bad religion, the way out of our repulsion is never to pit Jesus against the church, those called to Jesus and dedicated to him. There is an unalterable connection between Jesus and his people.

To separate Jesus from the church, based on his strong condemnation of bad religion, would be like saying that a homeowner who condemns and replaces mold-laden, sick-making drywall hates their home and family. To the contrary, the homeowner—who loves the family deeply and values the home they share—repairs that which has gone bad. The woes had a reparative goal in mind: halt and heal bad religion so that people were enabled to commit to the person and message of Jesus. In our day, ditching bad religion would be a sturdy and alluring on-ramp to faith.

Maybe the best way to think about the relationship between Jesus and the church is that Jesus, in his perfect love and inexhaustible wisdom, sees fit to pal around with imperfect people, to make such people some of his closest friends. Peter denied Jesus. Judas betrayed him. James and John wanted to call down the fire of judgment on unwelcoming cities. These four comprised a full one-third of his closest associates. Jesus treats you and me the same: we get to be near him in all our messiness while we grow in him.

This is a stunning grace, but there is a downside. We nurture criticisms regarding the way God has chosen to work among his imperfect people, to have flawed people flesh him out as his body, as the church. It is a stumbling block to faith. To find genuine, workable faith we must come to grips with this disappointment and confusion. We need to work through gloomy spiritual moments. The best way I can see to do this is to remain among the ranks of churchgoing people, bringing our imperfections with us, as together we find a home in Jesus, within the church.

Noting that members of the church are imperfect is a no brainer. It hardly needs to be said. But this is crucial: imperfection is never an excuse for serious, premeditated, abusive sin. It is one thing to slip and use a cuss word when you slice the end of your finger and not the celery—thereby sinning by letting an unwholesome word come out of our mouth (Ephesians 4:29; Colossians 3:8). It is quite another thing to consciously, with sinful intention, groom someone over a period of time for sex or to con them out of something, or to willfully lie about someone with the intent to destroy their reputation. Behaviors like those are not slip-ups, they are signs of a deeply troubled, un-Christlike conscience, of a troubled soul far from God, not really a part of the church, defined as those devoted to Jesus.

The church is the body of Christ (1 Corinthians 12:27; Romans 12:4-5). To join Jesus is to join the church. There is a permanent and unbreakable union between Jesus and those who are his own (John 6:39; 17:12; 18:9). We can't say we love Jesus and dismiss or hate the church. We can stumble over the sins of the church or have grave worries about what seem to be hypocritical inconsistencies. We can be troubled over her many sinfully fallen leaders. But for many people their ongoing conversion is a process with a two-pronged focus: (1) Growing in faith in Jesus while (2) forgiving the church, letting her off the hook and placing oneself humbly within the people of God.

## NAVIGATING AROUND BAD RELIGION

During the boarding process for a flight, I've occasionally found myself standing cramped with others in the entry way, near the cockpit door, and heard an alarmed, insistent, and adamant electronic voice:

Terrain, terrain! Pull up, pull up!

Those are the urgent words of the Ground Proximity Warning System (GPWS) on Boeing commercial aircraft. You never want to hear them midflight. But with the aircraft parked securely at the gate, the warning is heard every day, as pilots go through their preflight checklists.

The GPWS assists pilots with situational awareness. It lets them know where they are vertically with reference to upcoming terrain. Even with this great tool, in flight, pilots have less than a minute to avoid deadly terrain, to adjust their descent rate, or to respond to an unsafe clearance ahead. This is especially true when bad weather makes visibility impossible and pilots must fly with instruments only.

The rubble of bad religion diminishes spiritual visibility too. Sometimes we cannot see truth and goodness right in front of our face.

Jesus' scene was much like ours in the early twenty-first century: it was a landscape noted for its intellectual despair, re-lational brokenness, economic uncertainty, divisive political strife, and spiritual hopelessness. Into this reality came Jesus forming his community, proclaiming his message of hope. And the world has never been the same.

Is there ugly, scary religious terrain that must be circumnavigated? Yes. Does the church sometimes contribute to it? Yes. But overall, the one consistent light within the dark world has been Jesus and his true friends.

## JESUS THE HEALER

You will be comforted to discover that the founder of Christianity was not a promoter of bad religion. He was the cure for it. You can be sure that when Jesus challenged the religious leaders of his day, it was done in love-which-seeks-justice. Jesus sought the good purposes of God among the practices of bad religion. Jesus had a conscious agenda to be an agent of healing. His works of power in healing and deliverance were signs that a loving God was closely attuned to common, hurting people.

This is good religion. What we see in Jesus' conscious focus on healing shows the real heart of God. It reveals what life will be like once God's full justice has come in the renewed cosmos.

Jesus knew he had come to move God's story to that glorious end. But he also knew that in the middle of the story, most human beings feel far from God, not sure about prayer, and not confident about hearing his voice or receiving his guidance.

When Jesus healed, two things were being demonstrated: empathy and rightly used power. Jesus was a model of someone and something different from the other religious leaders of his day. His manner of being provided healing for bad religion. It gave hope for good religion.

## WOE TO RELIGIOUS LEADERS . . . AND SALVATION TO THOSE ABUSED BY THEM

Jesus, in his effort to correct and heal bad religion, had detailed criticism for the Jewish leaders who were his contemporaries (Matthew 23). Jesus accuses the teachers of the law and the Pharisees of not practicing what they preach (23:3). He says they tie up heavy, cumbersome loads and put them on other people's shoulders, but they themselves are not willing to lift a finger to move them (23:4). Jesus says everything they do is done for people to see (23:5). They love walking into a church, a board room, or a convention center and being invited to sit in places of honor, up front, in the spotlight (23:6). They love to be greeted with fancy titles that reinforce their superiority (23:7).

Rather than religious leaders separating themselves from the common folk, Jesus wanted them to identify with others as fellow students of the one Master Instructor: the Messiah (Matthew 23:8-10). Jesus thought the honorable way to be a religious leader was to be in alignment with his own simple, gracious, welcoming attitude expressed in Mark 10:45: he "did not come to be served, but to serve." For Jesus, unfussiness and humility, not complex religious structures and titles, compose the elegance and freedom of Christian spirituality, of good religion.

Most normal people of Jesus' day would have experienced—or would have known of a family member or friend who had experienced—the dysfunction of the bad religion he describes. People so harmed would have found in Jesus a fresh, freeing voice that reimagined religion and spirituality. Jesus was the embodiment of an attractive connection to God.

## SHUTTING THE DOOR TO GOD

Jesus said everyone who pursues Christian spirituality must "seek first the kingdom of God" (Matthew 6:33 ESV). People were trying, but the misguided leaders of bad religion were shutting the door of the kingdom in their face. Jesus said, "Woe to you, teachers of the law and Pharisees, you hypocrites! You shut the door of the kingdom of heaven in people's faces. You yourselves do not enter, nor will you let those enter who are trying to" (Matthew 23:13).

*The Message* puts it this way: "I've had it with you! You're hopeless, you religion scholars, you Pharisees! Frauds! Your lives are roadblocks to God's kingdom. You refuse to enter, and won't let anyone else in either" (Matthew 23:13 MSG).

Upon reading these woes we might think, "Wow, Jesus, what are you so upset about?!" "Oh, just this," he might respond, "I came to do one very specific thing: reveal the activity of God, the rule and reign of his kingdom on the earth. The expression of my Father's kingdom is the salvation and healing of all human sin and brokenness; all the pain, suffering, and death humanity groans under. And—ironically—bad religion is the most prominent hindrance to my work."

The religious leaders of Jesus' day failed to recognize the Messiah in their midst and refused to enter the kingdom he proclaimed. In so doing they hindered others coming to faith. They claimed to be teaching the truth but were in fact shutting the door of the kingdom in people's faces (Matthew 23:13-14). There could be nothing worse than working contrary to Jesus' stated intention: "I must proclaim the good news of the kingdom of God . . . because that is why I was sent" (Luke 4:43).

Jesus did not just proclaim kingdom truth, but he also healed as a sign of the inbreaking of the kingdom (Matthew 4:23). Further, Jesus said that "if I drive out demons by the finger of God, then the kingdom of God has come upon you" (Luke 11:20). Jesus' words and works were meant to announce, embody, and demonstrate God's good rule on behalf of humanity. When crowds heard Jesus teach, they were astonished at his profound insights into the most important matters of God and the human soul. This is a typical summary of the effect Jesus' ministry had on others: "The people were amazed at his teaching, because he taught them as one who had authority, not as the teachers of the law" (Mark 1:22).

Note the last line: *not as the teachers of the law*. The teachers of the law were doing their best to interpret the Old Testament story with the goal of ordering daily Jewish life. In this attempt they made ever-growing lists of strict, narrow laws. They made small laws to enforce the big laws, and even teenier laws to enforce the small ones. It is not hard to imagine how common folk were suffocated by their explanations of spiritualty. More important, these leaders were working at cross purposes with God.

The misguided leaders of Jesus' day twisted Scripture to create ways of saying one thing but doing another (Matthew 23:16-22). They were using clever-sounding ideas to appear moral while not being so. For instance, instead of "swearing by God," which was forbidden, they would swear by things associated with God: the temple, the altar, etc. We do similarly when we say, "I swear on a stack of Bibles!" It is far better, and a core part of good religion, to just be honest, to have no need to manipulate or control others by heaping vows on top of our claims to honesty. As Jesus taught, "Just say 'yes' and 'no.' When you manipulate words to get your own way, you go wrong" (Matthew 5:37 MSG).

Jesus thought the religious leaders of his day were doing more harm than good (Matthew 23:15). They were trying to win people to *their* ideas, *their* interpretations. Jesus thinks it is bad religion when religious teachers are not humbly seeking to teach what he taught, and do what he did, in the manner in which he did them. I know this is easier said than done. It is possible to differ on the meaning of Jesus' words. This is why these two words are vitally important: *humbly seeking*. When humility and diligent seeking are the core animating factors of religion, we might get off a stride or two, but we will not be making things worse by participating in bad religion.

## BAD RELIGION IS A HEAVY WEIGHT

Sally and Carter were struggling under the weight of this sort of bad religion. Do you remember the pain and confusion of their unanswered prayers? Each time a well-meaning person—making sure God was let off the hook—looked for a reason to blame them for their ineffectual prayers, they were being buried deeper in bad religion, their faith being suffocated by each shovelful of guilt-laden, shame-filled religion.

A classic moment in Jesus' life lays bare the conflict between the religious leaders and crowds of common folk like Carter and Sally:

A man who was demon-possessed and could not talk was brought to Jesus. And when the demon was driven out, the man who had been mute spoke. The crowd was amazed and said, "Nothing like this has ever been seen in Israel."

But the Pharisees said, "It is by the prince of demons that he drives out demons." (Matthew 9:32-34)

On a similar occasion, his protective heart worn bright and clear on his sleeve, Jesus revealed how serious he was about protecting common folk from bad religion:

> If anyone causes one of these little ones—those who believe in me—to stumble, it would be better for them to have a large millstone hung around their neck and to be drowned in the depths of the sea. Woe to the world because of the things that cause people to stumble! Such things must come, but woe to the person through whom they come! (Matthew 18:6-7)

This is the picture I want you to grasp: in the ancient equivalents of those who fill the honky-tonks on Broadway Street in Nashville, or who stroll the beaches of Southern California, or who slowly drive through the Northeast taking in the assorted vibrant colors of fall, or who live from paycheck to paycheck—the regular people—to them, Jesus, in stark contrast to the leaders of bad religion, was experienced as a loving, wise liberator. Bad religion binds and constricts humanity. Jesus unbinds and makes us free.

This experience of finding freedom in Jesus is a fundamental reason there has been a worldwide Jesus movement for two thousand years. That history is a major building block of confidence in the Spirit's ability to do the same today for those imprisoned by or done with bad religion.

To such people, to our own hearts, we cast the vision of liberty that comes from living in alignment with Jesus' vision and values. As the baffling fog of bad religion fades, the rubble in the religious terrain—both in the church and in our heart—will be perceived sooner and will be more manageable. Over time, as we absorb the genuine, the counterfeit fades away.

## THE BASICS OF GOOD RELIGION: JUSTICE, MERCY, AND FAITHFULNESS

Bad religion is an adventure in missing the point. That dynamic was at play between Jesus and the religious leaders. The religious leaders argued among themselves about the things they were supposed to pay tithes on. But they failed to take to heart the completely competent love, kindness, and wisdom of God's kingdom; therefore, they could not cultivate generosity of heart. They strained gnats (unclean creatures) from their lattes, while swallowing camels (another unclean creature) in their beer (Matthew 23:24).

They tripped over an aspect of bad religion called incidentals— the petty and peripheral—and missed that which is fundamental, central, and decisive.[2] In our day we might think of the person who would never use the N-word, but who also doesn't lift a finger to bring liberation to Black people and other people of color. Similar is the person who is always polite to others but who harbors hate in their heart.

The Jewish leaders of Jesus' day could not see what is important, or rather who is really important.[3] This massive distortion kept them from being generous, servant-hearted, cooperative friends of God who bring good religion—justice, mercy, and faithfulness—to their world.

### THE SPIRITUAL GENIUS OF JESUS

The leaders of religion who were contemporaries with Jesus misunderstood how spirituality is meant to work. They thought that faithfulness to God had mostly to do with externals (Matthew 23:25-26). Jesus, the master of virtuous, functional, love-of-others spirituality, knew that true religion was of the heart, the soul, the core aspects of humanity that motivate and animate our attitudes, actions, and words. He taught that "the things that come out of a person's mouth come from the heart, and these defile them. For out of the heart come evil thoughts—murder, adultery, sexual immorality, theft, false testimony, slander. These are what defile a person; but eating with unwashed hands does not defile them." (Matthew 15:18-20).

Jesus seems to be saying that good religion should have an intuitive element to it. Case in point: while picnicking at a river on the Sabbath, one shouldn't have to quote an ancient text as a rationale for scrambling into the water to rescue a drowning toddler—to *work* on the Sabbath. It is bad religion that fails to make good people who instinctually and immediately do the true good.

We read how badly Jesus' first hearers misunderstood him and we think, *We would have never stood in the crowd crying, "Crucify him, crucify him!"* (Luke 23:21). Working with two thousand years of reflection, we know better. We know how the story ends. The leaders of Jesus' day thought they had it right too (Matthew 23:29-32). They insisted, "We would never mistreat a prophet, much less murder them!" They protested, "We build monuments to them, for crying out loud!" But Jesus, similar to knowing that Peter would betray him (Luke 22:54-62), knew many of these very same people were already secretly plotting to put him out of business, even if it meant that politics, government, and religion—the mix of their nationalistic ambitions[4]—would need to come together to murder him.

It is both humble and wise to keep close to our heart the reality that bad religion is not far from any of us. Bad religion is easy, and true religion is a challenge.

## A BROOD OF VIPERS

Jesus summarizes his thoughts on the religious leaders of his day by calling them a brood of vipers—religiously evil and spiritually dangerous (Matthew 23:33). With that bold naming, a choice stands before us. Jesus was not like a nagging religious parent, nor did he behave like a manipulating evangelist. But he was always creating contrasts for the purpose of issuing a summons, presenting an invitation, and urgently calling for a decision. It is one thing to believe in Jesus—the game-changer is to believe him, to have so much confidence in what he taught and did that we choose to follow him instead of the vendors of bad religion.

"What will it be?," Jesus might say, "Will you follow me into true religion marked by a clean inner cup, into something more than a whitewashed tomb and curvy marks in a dusty path formed by a brood of vipers?" Jesus invites us to true religion which comes from the inside out and is most clearly seen not merely in religious activities, but in care for widows and orphans (James 1:27). That sort of religion is an appropriate mimicking of Jesus. He came to give his life, to draw all the power of sin and bad religion onto himself, paying the penalty for it and defanging it on the cross, opening by the love and grace of God a doorway though which we can walk, dropping our agendas, becoming humanity as God intended, ambassadors of good religion.

## THE LITTLE, LOVING CHURCH

I know it is hard to feel positive about most of the institutional expressions of church. I know that the hypocrisy and argumentative nature of the church hurts and troubles those who have given up on it. Thankfully, I have good news: throughout my long career supervising churches, I have seen, up close, many unknown churches whose members align to the vision and values of Jesus. They would be compelling to skeptics. You would be proud of them. They might wash away much maligning and fear of the church.

For instance, while as a teenager I was chasing sex, drugs, and rock-and-roll, the not-at-all-famous Methodist church I grew up in was caring for my mom who was suffering in a marriage dominated by the destructive, compulsive gambling of my father, leaving a mom with six kids and too little money for daily needs. I often wondered, *Why are those ladies—my mom's church mates— leaving bags of groceries on our front porch?* I also noticed, but could not have explained why, they sat in quiet conversation with mom for long hours.

I had no imagination that these ladies, these saints, were animated by the Spirit (love, kindness, and goodness [Galatians 5:22]) and were imitating Jesus—who came not to be served, but to serve (Mark 10:45). But they were. They were the little loving church that never shows up in the news. And that sort of unnoticed, selfless service is thousands of times more frequent than celebrity pastors who, abusing their power, engage in destructive sexual liaisons.

I know both sides. I've seen Christian leaders do just about every dumb and despicable thing imaginable. Yet, even today, my heart hurts when I hear about highly respected leaders, those "we could never imagine would do such and such." The embarrassment I experience is bad, but the erosion of hope, the thrashing of confidence that human beings can change, is worse. Yet, always quietly at work, demanding no headlines, is the little, loving church.

Having lived in and worked among the church for my entire life, I know this: the church is mostly composed of unknown people living quiet lives of faithfulness and dignity, loving Jesus, and serving others. If you've ever known someone like that, maybe they could become to you the true representative of Jesus' body—not the famous guy who just got caught viewing porn, stealing money, or abusing their position in order to sleep with the wrong person.

There are many legitimate positive observations about the church. Consider the thousands of hospitals and clinics for the poor or the myriad schools for the marginalized. The church has always been at the front and center of providing food and creating solutions for clean water and the healing hygiene that flows from it. When disaster strikes, it is often ordinary, unknown church people who respond—much to the surprise and delight of civic leaders and organizations like the Red Cross. The little loving church visits prisoners and works for prison reform. They are the main instrument for racial, economic, and spiritual healing in the world.

However, none of that is meant to be—nor could it be—a rationale for bad things that happen to people in church. Saying to victims of church abuse "not all Christians are bad" is re-wounding. It dismisses their specific experience in a deluge of well-meaning but defensive statistics. When a survivor of abuse reveals their courage by telling a person in power what happened to them, they are more afraid than most of us can imagine. In that moment, they simply want to hear,

- I am sorry . . .
- You did not deserve this . . .
- This is not your fault . . .
- You are treasured of God and my sister/brother in Christ . . .
- I see you . . .
- I hear you . . .
- I take your report seriously . . .
- In taking the next steps, I will help protect you from the perpetrator(s) . . .

That is precisely what the church should say. Sticking up for the down-and-out—isn't this what it means to know the Lord? (see Jeremiah 22:16 MSG).

Yet, back to the little, loving church, pause for a moment and look at something that shows the time: for me the clock is displaying 2:14 p.m. Got it? Next, consider that right now, this very instant, many of the more than two billion Christians spread across the world in every time zone are praying for the healing of the world and are engaged to that end in acts of kindness, justice, and peace. Multiple millions—at this very moment—are revealing the good religion of Jesus.

## EXERCISE
### APPLYING THE AIMS OF JESUS TO MY LIFE

1. Think of a couple specific ways people have harmed your trust in the church and hold them before God with the posture of the father in Mark 9:24: "I do believe; help me overcome my unbelief!" What do you sense God speaking to you in the mix of harm, belief, and unbelief? From within that mix, can you find faith to engage with Jesus' invitation, "I am willing"? Would you like to ask God to heal something specific in you?

2. From seeing Jesus in this chapter, what, if anything, about the person and character of Jesus stirs hope in you?

3. As a way to contemplate and soak in Jesus' good religion, recall a time when you or someone close to you received good, tangible care from those in a church body—home-cooked meals, financial support, childcare, assistance with house projects. Can you imagine yourself surrounded by and immersed in Jesus' good religion, animating and energizing you to be a source of good religion as well?

---

You might begin with this prayer:

*Jesus, I have complained much and long about my church hurts. I needed to process them, to think about them out loud with others. But along that way I have forgotten that you are the Healer. Please heal me. Please help me make amends with the people for whom I have been a source of bad religion. Bring your good religion to me and let it flow through me.*

What words of your own would you like to add?

# 8

# HOW CAN I FIND VIBRANT FAITH?

## JESUS' TEACHINGS POINT US TO A NEW WAY OF LIFE

*In him was life, and that life was the light of all mankind.*

**JOHN 1:4**

*Whoever loses their life for my sake will find it.*

**MATTHEW 10:39**

*By believing you may have life in his name.*

**JOHN 20:31**

**In the early 2000s** there was a car show called *Overhaulin'* featuring legendary car designer Chip Foose. In sixty minutes, viewers watched a falling-apart rust bucket found in a field, a garage, or a barn transformed into a work of automotive art. *Fixer Upper* is similar: in sixty minutes audiences get to follow along as Chip and Joanna Gaines purchase a rundown house in a nice neighborhood, fix it up, and turn it into a dream home.

Millions of people feel the same way about religion: it needs to be overhauled, fixed up.

Zach is a case in point. Sitting in our focus group, he did not stick out in any particular way. He seemed to like keeping himself to himself. His chair may have been pushed just slightly further from the table than others. But Zach was present, and if addressed, he would freely and warmly speak. He was thoughtful and had opinions, but he was never doctrinaire or inconsiderate.

We could tell when Zach was about to speak because his body preceded his vocal cords. He would slide back in his chair, his Levi's scraping against the upholstery, sit up straighter, and lift his head a bit. On one occasion, there seemed to be a bit of extra energy in his body language as he described his religious upbringing: "I was raised in a Unitarian Universalist Church. Though I no longer attend church, I consider myself spiritual. I am very interested in learning about God, and I seek spirituality through the lenses of many faiths. But my view of Christianity is spoiled by the historic and modern sins of the church—and by the sense I have that Christianity is flat and uninspired. It seems defensive and remote from real life."

After the session, people were squeezing by us in the cramped hallway. When there was a break in the procession, I asked Zach if he ever imagined a path out of his skepticism. He said, "It would have to involve an overhaul of what the extremes of organized religion have become—and that feels like a big task that I am not convinced could be achieved."

Zach longed for a vibrant religion that overflowed in a *good* way of life. The goodness of God and his kingdom is exactly what Jesus had in mind in his most appreciated body of teaching: the Sermon on the Mount. If Zach saw only rock-hard soil in which he would like to plant a beautiful rose bush of good religion, Jesus, similarly worked among hardhearted, confused, stubborn people who had lost hope that they could receive a vibrant faith, joining a religion that was for the good of the world.

That is the reality that gave rise to the Sermon on the Mount. In it, Jesus intended to teach a whole new way of living, the true religion and the authentic way of being human in the image and intention of God.

## JESUS' VISION FOR VIBRANT SPIRITUALITY

Jesus' critique of the religious vibe and practices of his contemporaries and his corresponding vision for good religion begins with the Beatitudes (Matthew 5:3-12). These sayings of Jesus reveal who is blessed, who is well off, and who has the good life. He next teaches that the people of God are meant to be truly good so that they will affect others in good ways—like being salt and light in and for the world (5:13-16).

Jesus' first hearers would have understood Jesus to be saying radical things that redefined important religious assumptions. Sensing this reaction in his hearers, Jesus assures the crowd, "Do not think that I have come to abolish the Law or the Prophets; I have not come to abolish them but to fulfill them" (Matthew 5:17). "Law" in Hebrew is *torah*. It is the revelation of God's wisdom. It is teaching that is meant to provide direction and guidance for how God wanted his people to live.

Jesus' hearers had wandered from the law as a way of life. They had turned it into mere religious observances that were no longer connected to God's purpose in giving the law—instruction for life as his people. Those who are skeptical of church in our day are criticizing modern Christianity for the same thing: too many religious attitudes and practices seem cut off from God and his good purposes on the earth.

Jesus knew he needed to guide the people listening to him on the mount away from mere rule keeping to engagement with God's purposes in giving the law in the first place: training for a way of life. That goal gave rise to him saying, "Unless your righteousness surpasses that of the Pharisees and the teachers of the law, you will certainly not enter the kingdom of heaven" (Matthew 5:20).

The Pharisees and teachers of the law were thought to be the best of Jesus' generation, having the highest commitment and deepest understanding of religion. However, these same people constantly harassed Jesus, frequently challenging his words and works. On one such occasion Jesus explained their behavior:

These people honor me with their lips,
> but their hearts are far from me.
They worship me in vain;
> their teachings are merely human rules. (Matthew 15:8-9)

Torah is of the heart, or it is nothing. Religion is of love, or it is truly annoying (1 Corinthians 13:1). The Bible analogies for this annoyance are a resounding gong or a clanging cymbal, the creaking of a rusty gate, just a noisy distraction (see 1 Corinthians 13:1 MSG, AMP). Religion not bathed in the life-shaping purpose of Torah, but rather steeped in religious rules, is a common reason people flee church and religion. It is lifeless. Not being rooted in love, it cannot do the true good. It can only approximate it. It's like eating my wife's sugarless candy: it's fine, but I immediately know "those aren't M&Ms!"

Jesus was shooting for the real thing. He imagined that authentic, good religion, cultivated in a heart of Jesus-like virtue, would naturally result in good words and good deeds—in a good life.

Jesus unpacks his way of life in several scenarios:

Should people congratulate themselves for keeping the law by not killing anyone today? No, they should cultivate a heart of love and self-sacrifice that makes murder inconceivable. (Matthew 5:21-22)

Should people keep religious observances while cultivating hate, condemnation, and retaliation in their heart? No, they should seek relational reconciliation from which good religion flows. Should hardhearted anger flow into lawsuits? No, strive to settle matters equitably. (Matthew 5:23-26)

Should we be happy with merely being against adultery "because the law says so?" No, Jesus' take on good religion says we should cultivate a heart that is not full of lust. (Matthew 5:27-30)

Should the church simply be angry at divorce as a source of social deterioration? No, we should nurture a heart that would not victimize a spouse for our own selfish pursuits. (Matthew 5:31-32)

Should religious people stop placing their hand on a Bible while vowing to tell the truth? Maybe, but Jesus' real point, contending for good and healthy religion, is that we should give up on spoken manipulation and verbal bullying. We should commit to simple, plain words, employing honest speech, letting our "yes" be yes and our "no" be no. (Matthew 5:33-37)

When someone harms us, should we hurt back in retaliation? Or do worse to them just to show them who is the boss and to prove that they should never mess with us again? No, we should, with appropriate vulnerability, keep our face, our other cheek in the game. This is not true in cases of abuse. An abused adult or child should never be told to "turn the other cheek."[1] What Jesus is getting at is that neighbor love, love of enemy, love of someone who has harmed us, requires, at a minimum, our presence, our cheek. Storming off can be the right thing to do to avoid further abuse, but often it is rationalized as a tool for retaliatory punishment, shunning people, for saying in effect, "I want nothing to do with you!" (Matthew 5:38-42)

If we discover we have an enemy—that is someone cursing us, hating us, or persecuting us—do we cyberstalk them, lob mean tweets in their direction, post embarrassing memes, or threaten to ruin them? Creating a shock to the human moral system, Jesus says to love your enemies; bless those that curse you; do good to those who hate you; pray for those who persecute you. (Matthew 5:43-47)

Jesus' vision for good religion is not rooted in moral philosophy, not in churchly rule keeping, not even precisely in Jewish religious history. Jesus knows about all that, but his stated purpose is that his hearers would respond to bad religion with good spirituality that mimics God's love for us, such that when bad things happen, we would "respond with the supple moves of prayer, for then you are working out of your true selves, your God-created selves. This is what God does. He gives his best—the sun to warm and the rain to nourish—to everyone, regardless: the good and bad, the nice and nasty" (Matthew 5:45 MSG).

Jesus summarizes all he has been teaching above with this conscious aim: "In a word, what I'm saying is, *Grow up.* You're kingdom subjects. Now live like it. Live out your God-created identity. Live generously and graciously toward others, the way God lives toward you" (Matthew 5:48 MSG).

In all this you can see that Jesus is a stunningly wise, good, and gracious teacher. Being the second person of the Holy Trinity, Jesus had the best insight possible about how citizens of the kingdom were meant to conduct their lives. He is the best, the greatest, the One to be most cherished. He is the head of a body that will one day perfectly receive and act on the signals and impulses that come from the head.

Until then, we groan (Romans 8:22). We stagger under the weight of the curse that came from the fall: physical pain, social anxieties, relational miseries, religious hypocrisy, frustrating division. We groan best, most fruitfully, when we groan together. And in the Jesus movement, together means church.

## HOW TO BE RELIGIOUSLY GOOD ACCORDING TO JESUS

Jesus taught a quiet, humble, unpretentious way of being religious. He believed that one's religion, one's prayer life, should never be exercised for selfish purposes or for the applause of others. He said the Father in heaven approves of and rewards this motive and manner of religion (Matthew 6:1-8).

Jesus presented a model for prayer that was rooted in the person and work of the Father: "may your name be greatly respected, revered, and honored; may you be esteemed as the truly Holy One." Jesus modeled and taught an orientation for all Christian spirituality that was embedded in wanting what God wants: "Your kingdom come, your will be done on earth [our realm] as it is in heaven [your realm]" (Matthew 6:9). Holding this basic worldview, Jesus then encourages us to trust our Father for our daily bread, for our forgiveness, for our ability to forgive those who have sinned against us—letting them off the hook, and finally to pray in confidence that God would not bring us to the time of trial, but rescue us from the evil one (6:9-13).

Jesus knew that forgiving those who have sinned against us is at the heart of good religion (Matthew 6:14-15). Much of what de-churched people reject has its roots in the bad behavior that flows from the need to retaliate, from the desire to punish. Those struggling to hold on to faith are often disheartened by seeing such behavior among Christians in their friendships, in marriages, between parents and children, in church boards, among church staff, and in small groups.

Jesus knew that forgiveness frees us from unattractive bitterness, hatred, and retaliation. He knew that those things pollute our soul and hinder the good we wish to do in the world. On the contrary, Jesus imagined the church finding a place of strength and goodness by naturally and routinely offering forgiveness. Jesus knew that forgiveness is the most logical, spiritual, and socially conscious way to live. Jesus knew, given the long history of bad religion that predated him, that living with hate and venomous anger is soul destroying for the one who refuses to offer forgiveness, and is also harmful to the one not forgiven. Jesus discerned that the unwillingness to forgive is a common bit of spiritual malpractice and is a prime source of bad religion.

Jesus next comments on one of the most frequent reasons people give for rejecting church: hypocrisy. Jesus says that employing hypocrisy has an intuitive reward: it can make people assume good things about us that are not true. Using fasting, which most people would see as an intense religious practice, Jesus teaches that the rewards that come from hypocrisy not only miss the real point of practicing religion, but they are also rewards that vastly pale in comparison to the reward given for genuine religion of the heart, which comes from a pure motivation to focus on God (Matthew 6:16-18).

The good feelings associated with tricking people into thinking we are something we are not is, in the wisdom of Jesus, an adventure in missing the point. Jesus knows posturing and pretending may be a way to get what we treasure on earth, but it is also the way we miss out on the more valuable and lasting treasures of heaven. Living in and through good religion encompasses a holism meant to express good religion, making our lives on earth heartfelt and honest, and thus good for others—and such lives are rewarded eternally by our Father in heaven (Matthew 6:19-23).

Jesus teaches that our eyes reveal the focus of our heart, our truest desires. From our eyes can be seen the aims of our words and our actions. Our authentic aspirations define whether our practice of religion is unhealthy darkness or full of light. Jesus knows that we can't have it both ways. "No one can serve two masters. Either you will hate the one and love the other, or you will be devoted to the one and despise the other" (Matthew 6:24).

*The Message* stimulates our imagination for what Jesus has in mind: "You can't worship two gods at once. Loving one god, you'll end up hating the other. Adoration of one feeds contempt for the other" (Matthew 6:24 MSG).

This is Jesus pressing a choice upon his hearers: What god do you seek? What will be first in your life, making everything else subordinate? Once we choose to derive our life from following Jesus and to live our lives according to his manner of being and his teaching, we achieve a major aspect of deliverance from human misery—worry (Matthew 6:25-32). Worry, as Jesus reveals, adds nothing to our life.

On the contrary, worry is often the motivation and accelerant for bad religion. Worry creates in us a fundamentally selfish posture focused on our fears and anxieties. Worry tends to make the people in our life problems to be fixed or vending machines for things we assume will comfort our stress: money, sex, nearness to power, amusement, etc. In that state of being, we are trapped. We are not free to pursue the good of others. We are not capable of embodying good religion.

Jesus is smart. He fully comprehended and empathized with human worry, anxiety, stress, and suffering. What did Jesus propose as the way to deal with all that? To deny it? No. To medicate it with sex, drugs, gambling, food, consumer goods? No. Rather, he taught that we should accept reality, while putting it in a secondary place. That raises a crucial spiritual question: What should be first in one's life so that the result is good religion? Jesus unveils that which is ultimate, primary, vital: "Seek first his kingdom and his righteousness, and all [the necessities of life] will be given to you as well" (Matthew 6:33).

*The Message* touches our heart with Jesus' meaning: "Steep your life in God-reality, God-initiative, God-provisions. Don't worry about missing out. You'll find all your everyday human concerns will be met" (Matthew 6:33 MSG).

## BUILDING BLOCKS FOR GOOD RELIGION

Jesus knew that judgmental attitudes were soul killing and community destroying (Matthew 7:1-2). A life marked by being judgmental is contrary to everything God intends for humanity as his agents of healing and freedom. That work cannot be done while having harsh opinions of everybody, or being constantly critical, or looking down on everyone around us.

How do we become more charitable, gracious, and generous in our views of others—and thus better positioned to be a fountain of good religion (Matthew 7:3-5)? Jesus says we should note what is real about us: we have a large plank of wood in our eye, blocking our vision, making an accurate verdict about others' tiny speck of sawdust impossible. Jesus wants us to see our need to deal with our blindness, with the partiality of our knowledge, to recognize that "we see through a glass, darkly" (1 Corinthians 13:12 KJV), that we are "squinting in a fog, peering through a mist" (13:12 MSG).

Our observations about others are clouded by the content of our memories and by the state of our heart and soul. Something unpleasant in our history can trigger unclear readings of other's motivations. Bias in our soul distorts our lens. Jesus is commending the self-awareness and humility needed to know that we perceive and evaluate others in ways that are so partial and uncertain that we should drop the habit of judgmentalism altogether. It kills good religion. It funds bad religion. It drives people from the Christian community.

Jesus' teaching about dogs, sacred things, pigs, and pearls (Matthew 7:6) has often been misunderstood and misused. It seems, given the audience to which the Sermon was addressed, that Jesus was saying to his Jewish hearers that they should not try to force Jewish religion onto Gentiles—especially not in terms that come from a Jewish worldview and culture. It will not make sense to Gentiles. The Gentiles will need to be approached on their terms, explaining the long story of Israel in terms they can understand and thus receive and benefit from.[2]

Dallas Willard shows how a misuse of Jesus' teaching is a common source of bad religion. The idea is simple: we can't push religion on others, whether or not they want it or are ready for it. If we try, we will only succeed in spreading bad religion. What motivates someone to push religion on others is worse than the act of doing it: we want to manage, to control the lives of others.[3]

Here is how bad religion spreads virulently: when people don't respond to our supposed superior insights the way we hoped they would, we get frustrated and might even condemn them. The point of Jesus' saying is not that some people ought to be judged as dogs or pigs—Jesus has just taught against such judgmentalism. What is in view here is not the *worthiness* of certain classes of people but the *helpfulness* of things we try to force on others on our terms and in our timing.

On the contrary, good religion leaves people freely in charge of their life before God. Jesus did not try to bring others under his control. He let the rich young ruler walk away. The woman at the well could have told Jesus *no*. Zacchaeus could have said he was too busy for dinner. Jesus never acted out of fear or a controlling attitude. He knew wheat and weeds would grow together and sheep and goats would be mixed in crowds until the day of judgment. Until then, he was at peace with how things were unfolding under the care of his Father. We can be too. If we do so, we will be a source of good religion.

The pursuit of and creation of good religion is simple: pray for God to enable you to live a life animated by the commitment to "in everything, do to others what you would have them do to you, for this sums up the Law and the Prophets" (Matthew 7:12). But this requires a choice: to walk down the wide street that is strewn with dysfunctional, judgmental bad religion or to walk with Jesus on the narrow way that is full of life, light, love, joy, and peace (7:13-14). Lots of voices will try to pull us toward bad religion (7:15-19). There is always some rationale for it available. But it produces bad fruit. Bad religion cannot nourish the soul. It makes the soul sick and then the sickness spreads to others.

## PUT MY WORDS INTO PRACTICE

Jesus comes to the end of the Sermon on the Mount like an evangelist calling for a decision (Matthew 7:24-27). He wonders if we will hear his words and put them into practice, thus creating a solid, stable life, an interior platform and capacity from which to do good, to be a model and source of good religion in public. Or will we hear his words and think of them as *nice* or *religious ideals*, but never try to live them, leading to an unstable existence that is not capable of withstanding the troubles of life? A wobbly person is self-focused, constantly trying to adjust to shifting sand. Such a preoccupied person has no capacity for others, no ability to spread good religion, no knack for being compelling to those who struggle with religion.

The crowds knew Jesus was something special. No other religious leader could match his personal goodness and stunning wisdom. Jesus was the opposite of what they experienced with the leaders of misguided, bad religion. Matthew tells us that "when Jesus had finished saying these things, the crowds were amazed at his teaching, because he taught as one who had authority, and not as their teachers of the law" (Matthew 7:28-29).

I too am amazed at Jesus. Having considered him up close for decades, he grows more magnificent in my heart and mind every day. I am especially encouraged when I see the Jesus life lived out in others. In that sense we are all similar to de-churched people: our hearts constantly range about looking for signs of good religion in the lived reality of human beings.

## CORACLE

One model of good religion is my friend and colleague Bill Haley. Bill has discovered and lives the way of Jesus. He is an Anglican priest who serves with me on the board of advisers for the Center for Formation, Justice and Peace.[4] Bill is also the founder of Coracle.[5] A *coracle* is a small, oval-shaped, lightweight boat that is tailored to local contexts, particular river conditions, and the unique needs of an individual boat user.

Coracle invites people into the way of Jesus, to share in the life of Jesus while we're in the world—to incarnate the incarnation.[6] Bill's passion is to assist people in formation into Christlikeness for the sake of being loving, healing, redemptive instruments for God in our broken world. This is a rich, joyful, challenging way of life. It is humanity as God envisioned us.

Coracle emphasizes working for reconciliation with God and each other, including peacemaking, racial healing, justice, and creation care. This is the heart of good religion. Jesus' way of life as expressed in the Sermon on the Mount is the final form of the divine dynamism expressed in Adam and Eve, who were invited to work with God, tending his creation (Genesis 2:15) and of the calling of Abraham and the creation of Israel to be a blessing to the whole world (Genesis 12:1-3).

Motivated by Jesus' teaching "blessed are those who mourn," on Juneteenth of 2020—a few weeks after George Floyd was killed—Coracle, in partnership with eighteen other churches and ministries, sponsored a Lament for Racial Injustice. Because of Covid-19 restrictions, it was broadcast from the Corhaven Graveyard, a burial ground for twenty-five enslaved African Americans in Virginia's Shenandoah Valley. Five hundred people participated. It was meant to comfort, give strength, and assist in racial healing. It was good religion on display.

Good religion is the truth. Bad religion is an impostor. Good religion is the design feature, bad religion is a flaw. We can step into the flow of good religion any time we want—we simply step into our coracle and flow along in the way of Jesus.

## EXERCISE
### APPLYING THE AIMS OF JESUS TO MY LIFE

1. What is your perspective of Jesus as a *teacher*? Guitarists would love to learn from Eric Clapton, B. B. King, or Chuck Berry. Soccer players would give just about anything to learn from David Beckham, Lionel Messi, Briana Scurry, or Mia Hamm. Do you have the same intuitive respect for the teaching of Jesus? Why or why not?

2. If not, what circumstances have led you to question whether the teachings of Jesus are a sturdy foundation? Can you also name some of the ways your faith has been grounded in the teachings of Jesus? How have these experiences concretized the way of Jesus for you?

3. Do you believe Jesus' teachings are the foundation for good religion—that conformity to them is the way to have a firm, stable, sustainable life on solid rock? Why or why not? How do you sense God might be inviting you to return to the genius and goodness of Jesus' words in your current context?

---

You might begin with this prayer:

*Jesus, I have known you as Savior. Today I receive you as my Master Teacher. I need your insights for every aspect of my life. I want to be your apprentice in kingdom living as you taught and modeled it. I want in on life as you describe it. I want to be a fountain of good religion. My desire is to be your agent of healing in the world.*

What words of your own would you like to add?

# 9

# WHY IS CONSISTENT SPIRITUAL GROWTH SO DIFFICULT?

## JESUS' EMPHASIS ON THE CENTRALITY OF THE HEART

*These people honor me with their lips,*
*but their hearts are far from me.*

**MATTHEW 15:8**

*Out of the heart come evil thoughts—murder, adultery,*
*sexual immorality, theft, false testimony, slander.*

**MATTHEW 15:19**

*A good man brings good things out of the good stored up in his heart,*
*and an evil man brings evil things out of the evil stored up in his heart.*

**LUKE 6:45**

"I *guess* so."

That was Charlotte's way of agreeing to speak with me when she was in fact not so keen on the idea. In one of my group interviews, as we went around introducing ourselves and our current connections to church or Christianity, Charlotte described herself as barely hanging in with Christianity because she was deeply frustrated by how little fruit was shown through her long and sincere attempts at spiritual growth. In various phases of her life, she had tried Bible reading programs, prayer guides, devotional books, women's groups, and retreats.

Given the setting of a one-time conversation with a socially mixed group of guests, not a long-standing group of spiritual friends, I was impressed with her openness. Like an animal trying to shake free from a pestering bug, she described wanting to be liberated from what she described as characteristic and too frequent outbursts of anger toward her kids and coworkers. She was also disturbed by hate that was frequently just below her visible life. She described instinctual condemnation of those she thought were messing up the world. She wondered aloud, "Also, why do my bad desires and sinful impulses never seem to go away? Why I am I always fighting them?"

The formal conversation over, some in the group were grabbing their jackets and umbrellas and heading out the door into a rare rainstorm in Southern California. But most were hanging around the room, eating and drinking, hoping the rain was just a passing shower. As Charlotte finished a conversation, I took the opportunity to ask if she would meet with me to help me better understand her spiritual frustration.

Charlotte's office was just one exit down the freeway from my office, so she agreed to come see me after work at a later date. When the day arrived, she appeared promptly at 5:15. We were mindful that traffic would only increase in the next hour and that we both needed to get home to dinner with our families, so we sat down quickly and began our conversation.

Charlotte began by asking if she could share something she didn't say in the group. "Of course," I answered. "I am grateful for your willingness to help me understand religious frustration."

Taking a breath, her eyes widening a bit, she said with a declarative tone, "I'm so bummed by the contrast between my most instinctive inner drives and my vision for being a healthy spiritual woman. If anybody ever found out what I really thought, I would be aghast! The things that sometimes flit through my mind even trouble me. I can't imagine how harshly I might be judged and soundly rejected if others knew my unspoken contemplations. None of my approaches to spiritual transformation have worked over the long haul. And when they do seem to work, I either feel like it is grudging religious obedience, not wholehearted; or, because of my doublemindedness, I judge it to be tinged with hypocrisy. I just couldn't keep living with that frustration, that inner angst, so I pretty much threw in the towel a couple years ago."

Our conversation of discovery concluded and silence companioned us as we walked down the concrete stairs to our cars—until a thought struck me. I thought it might inspire Charlotte. As I tossed my backpack into the trunk, I called out, "Charlotte, next time let's talk about the genius of Jesus, his fundamental insight that true, good religion is of the *heart*. He taught a lot about it. In fact, we could call the worldwide movement he started a revolution of the heart."

## TRUSTING WHAT JESUS TAUGHT

I have empathy for people who can't respond well to the truth claims of religion. Like a turtle on a fence post, they did not get there on their own. Like Charlotte, some hurtful experience or deep disappointment landed them on a suspicious, cynical post-of-life. For our purposes in this book, knowing and aligning with the aims of Jesus comes down to this: *Would you like to take the hand offered to you by Jesus and get off your fence post?* Would you like there to be someone who knows truth and who works with it in nonbullying, nonmanipulative servant love, aiming at the ultimate, good purposes of God?

We often say, "Well, I know he did that, or she said that, but really she or he has a good heart." With that phrase we mean to convey that one verbal outburst or a single moment of sin does not fully define a person. True. And I recognize that the impulse behind the saying is kindness, of not wanting to be judgmental, of giving space for second chances, for opportunity for growth. All that is commendable.

But the saying is unhelpful in that it disconnects outward behavior from the place from which words and deeds come: one's heart.

Most all of us would be offended if it were suggested that something was wrong with our heart, with our essential self, our internal being. We commonly begrudge it, but God is always looking at the heart. Dallas Willard, my friend and mentor, made issues of the heart central to his explanation of Christian spirituality. Seeking to live and teach from within the worldview of Jesus' revolution of the heart, Dallas wrote a well-received book called *The Renovation of the Heart*. In it, we hear Dallas echo Jesus:

> The revolution of Jesus is in the first place and continuously a revolution of the human heart or spirit . . . [it] is a revolution of character, which proceeds by changing people from the inside through ongoing personal relationship to God in Christ and to one another. It is one that changes their ideas, beliefs, feelings, and habits of choice, as well as their bodily tendencies and social relations. It penetrates to the deepest layers of their soul.[1]

Actions are not impositions on who we are, but are expressions of who we are. They come out of our heart and the inner realities it supervises and interacts with.

> [Jesus] saves us by realistic restoration of our heart to God and then by dwelling there with his Father through the distinctively divine Spirit. *The heart thus renovated and inhabited is the only real hope of humanity on earth.*[2]

Jesus' revolution of the heart is both loving and wise:

The hidden dimension of each human life is not visible to others, nor is it fully graspable even by ourselves. We usually know very little about the things that move in our own soul, the deepest level of our life, or what is driving it. Our "within" is astonishingly complex and subtle—even devious. It takes on a life of its own. Only God knows our depths, who we are, and what we would do.[3]

Religion reduced to willpower or determination commonly leads to bad religion. Striving to do the right thing, while other, definitive aspects of our being are bent in the opposite direction, does not result in real change, in good religion. It creates constant disappointment, frustration, and anger in people, who too often take out their annoyance on others.

In part, this explains how people reacted to the Pharisees and other religious teachers of Jesus' day. They did not experience religious leaders as winsome or attractive. Jesus was. Why? Jesus, from his heart, lived and modeled good religion. Though intently focused, he radiated space-making hospitality, goodness, kindness, grace, generosity. Everyone saw in him stunning religious power that was always in service to the good of others—his healing, deliverance, and wise teaching freed people spiritually instead of constricting their lives religiously.

Merely focusing on one's will, willpower, or inner fortitude is not a reliable long-term method for living within Jesus' revolution of the heart. Our wills are constantly badgered by our thoughts, feelings, and social interactions. Something needs to sort out that tension, that inner argument and give us a consistent, dependable way of being. That is the role of the heart. As Dallas is quoted as saying, "The aim of spiritual formation is not behavior modification but the transformation of all those aspects of you and me where behavior comes from; it is a circumcision of the heart."

Thus,

> the greatest need you and I have—the greatest need of collective humanity—is renovation of our heart. That spiritual place within us from which outlook, choices, and actions come has been formed by a world away from God. Now it must be transformed.

Indeed, the only hope of humanity lies in the fact that, as our spiritual dimension has been *formed*, so it also can be *transformed*.[4]

## GOOD RELIGION FROM THE HEART

From town to town, Jesus walked and conversed with people who misunderstood God and his intent for humanity. Though expressing itself in various ways, misinterpreting Jesus was common for Jews and non-Jews alike. Jesus' teachings about the heart were primarily aimed at the Jews. His goal was to help them see that their religion had become something external, a grudging drudgery that was not of the heart. Their hearts, their most genuine desires, their truest affections were not in it. This external, legalistic approach to religion was a big turnoff. The moralistic pressure regular people felt from religious leaders "went viral," as we say, becoming a pandemic of bad religion.

Jesus comes along and reveals that there is a better way, a good approach to religion that spreads goodness to others. Good religion comes from a transformed heart. Jesus teaches that the heart is something like the CEO of the self, the soul, the person-in-whole. It bosses our bodies, attitudes, words, and actions. This is what Jesus means when he teaches, "You brood of vipers, how can you who are evil say anything good? For the mouth speaks what the heart is full of. A good man brings good things out of the good stored up in him, and an evil man brings evil things out of the evil stored up in him" (Matthew 12:34-35).

There was a time when the Great Lakes of the upper Midwest were a toxic soup. One might say "nothing good could come from there." You would not have wanted to eat the fish or drink the water. Jesus is saying something similar about the heart: from a good lake comes nutritious fish and clean thirst-quenching water. From a bad one comes dead fish and polluted water.

There are many sources of bad religion. But good religion has only one: transformation of the heart in the way of Jesus.

Why do otherwise well-intentioned people persist in external-only religious practices? Because in their religious systems, they need to know who is in and who is out. Sometimes being in is judged by one's beliefs, but most the time it is determined by outward behavior. The leaders of bad religion check up on these things.

On one occasion, an official delegation was sent from Jerusalem to examine Jesus and his revolution. They were the best trained and most highly respected teachers in the land. They were revered, but remote leaders, rigid in enforcing far-reaching religious rules. It seems trivial to our ears, but for the devout religious people of Jesus' day breaking one of the ceremonial laws—like handwashing—was a serious offense (Matthew 15:1-20).

At issue in that situation was identifying who was accurately representing God: the teachers of the law or Jesus? Whose way of life honors and aligns with God and his purposes in creation?

Being seen to be in the right brings power. The establishment of power and authority with the people was the real underlying religious tension between Jesus and his critics. An undeniable sort of power is in play when religious leaders monitor and insist on certain behaviors. On the contrary, Jesus' gospel of the kingdom challenges the human heart. It goes inside to create changes that do not need external forces to manage them. These changes in behavior become natural, organic, not pretended or forced. Jesus proclaimed a mode of spirituality that transformed motives, desires, and aspirations. It was meant to produce good Christianity, rooted in accurate discernment of the inner self, married to a lifestyle of repentance, seeking to change anything in one's inner reality that is malformed.

In the case at hand, the Pharisees and scribes were noting external behavior: Jesus' students were not washing their hands ceremonially before they ate. Doing so was a daily, social marker of religious adherence. But Jesus was leading a different sort of movement. His was a kingdom-based revolution of the heart. In their view, this made Jesus dangerous.[5] But Jesus was never seeking to set God's commands or teachings (the law) aside; he was always teaching about the kind of life and modeling the sort of person the law was meant to produce.

Jesus' response to the query about handwashing reveals the error of external religious practices that are divorced from the heart goals of good religion:

Why do you break the command of God for the sake of your tradition? . . . You nullify the word of God for the sake of your tradition. . . .

[You] honor me with [your] lips,
    but [your] hearts are far from me.
[You] worship me in vain;
    [your] teachings are merely human rules.
        (Matthew 15:3-9)

This moves the conversation from religious tradition to the core lifestyle the law was meant to inspire—love of and obedience to God, the overflow of which is seen in two primary ways: loving one's neighbor and loving one's enemy. Jesus is teaching the religious leaders that their tradition of external religion was leading them to transgress the very law they insist they were upholding. But in fact, they were missing by a mile the law of love and generosity to others. Jesus says this is hypocritical, that their real heart devotion was not where their attestations say it was. God is not interested in the religious image created by one's lip service or public posturing. He is interested in what is real, what is at the center of our being, what is in our heart.

Jesus explicitly described what he intended as the essential outcome of his teaching: "'Love the Lord your God with all your heart and with all your soul and with all your mind.' This is the first and greatest commandment. And the second is like it: 'Love your neighbor as yourself'" (Matthew 22:37-39).

In the Matthew 15 passage we've been thinking about, Jesus is using that core paradigm to probe the hearts of the religious leaders: You don't really honor your father and mother as the fifth commandment teaches; you find feigned rationales based in religious tradition for hanging on to all your money so that it is not available to help your parents in their old age—which would be a very low bar for what it means to honor one's parents. You are like sneaky accountants finding questionable loopholes to avoid paying rightfully owed taxes (Matthew 15:3-6).

Parents are among the closest of all possible neighbors. To use religious loopholes to withhold assistance from them is to transgress all that Jesus taught. It is to reveal a fundamentally selfish heart being hidden by external religious practice. It is to say no to Jesus' revolution that is meant to bring purity to the full depth of the heart. Jesus was offering deep transformation from inner impurity. The teachers and practitioners of bad religion were focused on religious ritual that had come untethered from the purposes of God. Jesus' focus was not on unwashed dirty hands, but on heart issues that need a good scrubbing.

The apostle Paul was deeply committed to the Jewish religious practices of his heritage. But upon conversion, his whole outlook changed. He became a powerful spokesperson for finding good and true religion among the mess of bad religion:

Since you died with Christ to the elemental spiritual forces of this world, why, as though you still belonged to the world, do you submit to its rules: "Do not handle! Do not taste! Do not touch!"? These rules, which have to do with things that are all destined to perish with use, are based on merely human commands and teachings. Such regulations indeed have an appearance of wisdom, with their self-imposed worship, their false humility and their harsh treatment of the body, but they lack any value in restraining sensual indulgence. (Colossians 2:20-23)

Paul knows religious rules never reach or transform the heart. Paul recognized that some people "claim to know God, but by their actions they deny him" (Titus 1:16). Washing hands was a way of publicly claiming, "I know God." Failing to care for one's parents was to deny God and his purposes for his people.

If religious traditions help us embody virtuous spirituality, then great, adopt them. If not, ditch them, or adjust your interaction with them. People who are fed up with stunted spiritual growth are trying to do just that. It is best not to judge them—or judge ourselves—in their process. Rather, rejecting fear, controlling instincts and manipulation, we are called to companion frustrated de-churched people along the way, expressing patient support and easygoing encouragement. For an imagination of this, think of the patience Jesus had for his first twelve followers. When they were under the load of bad religion, he was an easy yoke. When they were heavily wrong, he was a light burden.

## A RADICAL CURE

To err means to make a mistake, to be inaccurate, or to have an oversight in thinking, judgment, or conduct. The word comes from a Latin word that means "to stray." This leads me to think of the Hebrew terms for *sin* in the Old Testament—the most common refer to being or doing that which is contrary to God's nature, morally wrong, or crooked or twisted with reference to the path laid out by God. *Sin* also refers to transgressions rooted in rebellion against God and his aims; or to an offense against the person of God, making one guilty before him.

But error and sin are not the only options for life. They do not describe the totality of human reality. There are antidotes for error: people find and live truth; people come to grips with reality; they see and respond accurately; they are guided by correct ideas and respond to God in obedience.

Hebrew vocabulary in the Bible knows of this human reality. This way of life is described by the word *righteousness*. It designates one who is upright and conscientious in their behavior, who is on the straight path, who does not depart from the way of God, who is just in their dealings with others, and who is thus seen to be in the right.

Now picture Jesus before any crowd. He knows that the people in the crowd live in various mixes of sin and error, righteousness and truth, having both pure and polluted hearts. Within this typical human predicament Jesus never acts like a nag, harassing and irritating people. He functions like a prophet, brokenhearted at the spiritual condition being observed, saying, "I see what is real and true; you cannot see it, but trust me, I have come to clean the windshield of your mind so you can see the road, the way, and get back on it." Jesus's words and actions reveal his passionate aim:

- God did not send his Son into the world to condemn the world, but to save the world through him. (John 3:17)

- I've come to start a fire on this earth—how I wish it were blazing right now! I've come to change everything, turn everything right-side up—how I long for it to be finished! (Luke 12:49 MSG)

- I came into the world to bring everything into the clear light of day, making all the distinctions clear, so that those who have never seen will see, and those who have made a great pretense of seeing will be exposed as blind. (John 9:39 MSG)

Jesus knew that people like Zacchaeus and the woman caught in adultery did not need a public religious spanking for moral failures, but rather salvation on the order of rescue and deliverance from that which bound them to heart habits that led to sin. Jesus knew that most people felt self-condemnation even if they could not fully identify it or articulate it. To all varieties of individuals, with various ways of religious thinking, or no consideration of religion at all, Jesus aimed to impart life. His aspiration was to be light and power that led humankind out of the fear, pain, and hopelessness that causes so many desperate and sinful measures to be inflicted on others by the hands, and out of the mouths, of human beings.

Ben Meyer wrote, "For Jesus, his aims equal his vocation; they gave focus to his purposes and animated and guided his performances, his words and deeds. This is the pattern or form or determining principle of Jesus' career."[6] Meyer quotes T. W. Manson as saying, "Jesus' vocabulary, themes, tone and point differ depending on to whom he is conversing. . . . But in every case, Jesus is always calling for 'a radical cure for hardness of heart.'"[7]

## CONSTRUCTING AFTER DECONSTRUCTING

I empathize with people like Charlotte. I often share her frustration with the halting and slow nature of my spiritual growth, with the fear that accompanies it: What if I am stuck with myself and cannot change? In addition, I am apprehensive that church systems, having their own external institutional concerns and aims, are capable of hosting and facilitating the revolution of Jesus.

Recently, however, I have found some hope from my friend and colleague, Scot McKnight, a distinguished New Testament scholar. Scot wrote in his newsletter that when spiritually struggling people become de-churched, begin deconstructing their faith, hit bottom, and then begin reconstructing their faith, the first building blocks are captured in three terms: *Jesus*, *justice*, and *example*.

**Jesus.** Nearly everyone intuits that Jesus and the institutional church are often at odds. This explains the "dones." They are done with church but trying to find the real Jesus.

**Justice.** Reconstructing faith almost always includes a rethinking of all the implications of salvation. Not so much in "how is it achieved"—the emphasis of previous generations—but what does it encompass, who is it for, how does the church cooperate with God to implement it? Once people begin to ask those sorts of questions, they realize that salvation includes deliverance, healing, and rescue—justice—for all that ails humanity.

**Example.** Scot quotes Douglas Campbell, professor of New Testament at Duke Divinity School: "The answer for Christian communities is that we should have Christian leaders who are characterized by the relational qualities that we want everyone else to copy. He gets this right. A kind of 'show me' that is more important than 'tell me.'"[8]

Scot further writes, "*Reconstructors* aren't 'joining' any group on the basis of its beliefs. If they join in, it is on the basis of a group's behaviors. Dietrich Bonhoeffer, who in Tegel's prison was looking beyond deconstruction to reconstruction, said it this way about the future of the church beyond the war: 'the church's word gains weight and power not through concepts but by example.'"[9]

## RISE TO READ

I heard Gabrielle Beam speak at a pastor's conference. She is a graduate of Yale University who describes herself as Native American, African American, and European Jew. Her sweetness of spirit, strength of character, and bold intelligence shined forth as she articulated her passion to stamp out early childhood illiteracy and break the cycle of poverty among children. These kids have the cards stacked against them from the beginning. They are told from early childhood that they will be nothing. I can't have been the only one in the room deeply moved as Beam described how the hearts of these children are malformed by their daily reality. But Beam is not content with description; she works toward renovation.

Beam moves others because she was first moved by a combination of the biblical vision for doing good and the harsh realities faced by too many children. Deuteronomy 30:19 spoke to her clearly: "This day I call the heavens and the earth as witnesses against you that I have set before you life and death, blessings and curses. Now choose life, so that you and your children may live."

Beam knew by observation and analysis of her neighborhood that many children were not really living, that she would have to choose life for herself in order to bear life on their behalf. Only about one-tenth of the children in her sphere of influence could read even at a second-grade level. She says that upon seeing this reality, she was flung out of the church by God and into the mission field of poor urban spaces. Later, during a phone interview, she explained to me that 60 percent of the children in her city who graduate from high school are functionally illiterate, and that poor reading skills are a prime predictor of incarceration rates. Rise to Read uses the Bible to teach reading. In this way it is both practical and spiritual. Parents and school administrators love the outcomes the program achieves.

Beam is determined to break the school-to-prison pipeline. Why? She is part of Jesus' revolution of the heart. Her heart was changed by Jesus and empowered by the Holy Spirit. In our interview, she recounted the privilege her family enjoys. Her husband is a PhD physicist. Her children attended Stanford. One

day the kids were inquiring about her commitment to poor, illiterate children. Beam replied, "The only difference between you
and the kids in Bridgeport is opportunity and exposure. I want to
give these kids as much of a break as possible. I want them to
experience the potential that lies in them. I want them to get in
on Jesus' revolution of the heart."

As I sat in Beam's audience, imagining the work of God in and
through her, good religion washed over me and the whole crowd.
Hope was kindled. We got a glimpse of the truth that through
Jesus' revolution of the heart, good deeds, justice, and good religion are possible.

## EXERCISE
### APPLYING THE AIMS OF JESUS TO MY LIFE

1. Name an area or two where, despite your best efforts to
   change, transformation still eludes you. In what ways have
   you relied on willpower to change these habits of the heart?
   How might the notion of a renovation of the heart in the
   way of Jesus invite you to deeper layers of understanding
   your actions?

2. What hidden dimension of your being most needs to be
   renovated right now? Just notice—remembering that self-
   condemnation is not the way of Jesus—and invite the Spirit
   into your discernment.

3. How would you describe your personal hunger and motivation for a truer representation of Jesus in your current
   context? How do you imagine such renovation flowing out
   of you for the good of others?

You might begin with this prayer:

*God, I can see now that I have missed the path to spiritual
growth. Seeing the Jesus revolution, I desire the renovation of*

*my heart, the transformation of my soul. I welcome you and I invite you probe the depths of my being, transforming me from the inside out. Seeking to experience good religion and to be an agent of it, I give myself to your revolution of transformed hearts.*

What words of your own would you like to add?

# 10

# IS THERE AN AUTHENTIC COMMUNITY OF FAITH?

## JESUS INTENTIONALLY CALLED AND SENT A PEOPLE

*Jesus went out and saw a tax collector by the name of Levi sitting at his tax booth. "Follow me," Jesus said to him, and Levi got up, left everything and followed him.*

**LUKE 5:27-28**

*As you go, proclaim this message: "The kingdom of heaven has come near." Heal the sick, raise the dead, cleanse those who have leprosy, drive out demons. Freely you have received; freely give.*

**MATTHEW 10:7-8**

*Go out and train everyone you meet, far and near, in this way of life, marking them by baptism in the threefold name: Father, Son, and Holy Spirit. Then instruct them in the practice of all I have commanded you. I'll be with you as you do this, day after day after day, right up to the end of the age.*

**MATTHEW 28:18-20 MSG**

**Whenever I've observed a child** shaping Play-Doh in their hands, I wonder, *What will they form?* Sometimes they tell me they've made a dog, but it looks more like a cow, or that they've made Grandpa, but the clay figure looks more like Gumby.

Similarly, everyone has an idea about what shape of church and Christianity should emerge from God's hands. We have opinions about what kind of person a Christian ought to be and what character the church ought to have. These oughts are powerfully suggestive. They form the basis by which we judge each other and judge the church. Many de-churched people have tripped and lost their faith over an ought or should.

Recently, a beloved lifelong friend died. My wife and I and a few mutual friends were not able to attend the funeral, so to celebrate her life we organized a reunion at a rustic but comfortable mountain cabin, well stocked with favorite snacks and hot drinks we could bring around a warming fire. As we reminisced about decades of friendships that were created and deepened at our church, we recalled several friends who were now done with the whole thing in the wake of failed marriages and lack of support from the church community.

Here are some of their stories.

Molly felt let down by God when her husband, a very successful businessman, had an affair with a coworker. Not long after came the shocking and heart-wrecking death of her teenage son. Her disappointment with God increased during an unjust divorce settlement. She has not been to church in decades.

Harper's husband was a simple and delightful man until mental illness overtook him and he attempted a most brutal suicide in plain view of one of his children. Harper divorced her husband. One of her children became a drug addict and overdosed. When her own mental health began to decline, it was the last straw, and she concluded, "God does not love me or protect me." She lost all desire and energy for going to church, for being around people she feared might judge her or attempt to give sympathy that she was not ready to receive.

Brooke's husband served the church his whole life. He seemed to be an icon of the perfect, caring pastor. And in many ways, he was. Innumerable people testified to the care he had shown them. But he betrayed Brooke though multiple affairs while overseas on ministry trips and with a staff person. Brooke, deeply loving the people at church, had been like a mother to many. But when her husband's sin became public and the church had to deal with it, things got awkward. Warm smiles turned to uncomfortable greetings in which no one knew what to say. She felt like her husband's sin was ruining her life at church. It was all so unfair. Where was God? Brooke hung in for years, but through watching church services at home during the Covid-19 shutdown, she finally found a way to stop attending church.

Sitting around the fire, our friend Mike shared his own response, "I totally get our friends being done with church. I don't judge them a bit. But I wonder, even with all the crud we have experienced over the years, does there remain some solid, true explanation for our hunger for a community of good religion?"

## HOW WAS CHURCH?

I don't know how to answer these questions anymore: How was church? Was church good? I don't mean to suggest the questions are bad or wrong. I think the problem is me. I don't expect church to be good anymore. I am not even sure what the question means except maybe, "Was the worship music emotionally moving and did the sermon match my political persuasions?"

Church for me has become a weekly practice within my overall spiritual disciplines. Put in that category, maybe my feelings make better sense. Prayer is not great every morning—some mornings are way more inspired than others. Bible reading is not always a mountaintop experience, but some days I would swear a given passage was written for me, in my situation, meeting my deepest needs. Not every retreat, time of silence, or day of solitude is identically vibrant, but some change our lives.

Church services are like that too. We should not put so much pressure on them. As an aside, the consumeristic pressure we put on church is really heaped on the staff and lay leaders. They bear some responsibility in it, but our pressure on them is a root cause of the burnout we see all around us.

I am fortunate to go to a liturgical church.[1] The elements of our worship include, but go far beyond, singing, offering, announcements, and a message. We confess our sins and hear absolution. We affirm the Nicene Creed as the outline of our story, giving shape and meaning to our life. We pray for the whole world as a whole people. We touch each other with a hug or fist pump as we pass Christ's peace to one another. We receive Eucharist as one people around one table at which Jesus is host. Those are now spiritual practices for me. They don't need to be perfect or even good, they just need to be there in a community of other followers of Jesus.

I am trying to die to consumerist tendencies about church. And I don't expect the people in church to be perfect. But church still matters as a set of practices and relationships that empower my desire to follow Jesus and participate in the story of God that is coming true in and through him.

## PARTICIPATING WITH GOD

For all of us—churched, barely churched, or de-churched—this reality stands: Jesus sent his followers out to carry on his kingdom work, and he expected them to do it. This is primarily a relational reality, not merely pragmatic or utilitarian. God, unlike what is often seen in church leadership, is not (negatively construed) *using* his people. He invites us to participate in his ongoing work. The vocation of the church is rooted in God's own life and action in the world. The church comprises those people who obediently live out the life of the rule and reign of God. The people of God being present in day-to-day life as the cooperative friends of God is what it means to be light, to be the goodness that my friends around the fire are looking for.

Jesus said:

You're here to be light, bringing out the God-colors in the world. God is not a secret to be kept. We're going public with this, as public as a city on a hill. If I make you light-bearers, you don't think I'm going to hide you under a bucket, do you? I'm putting you on a light stand. Now that I've put you there on a hilltop, on a light stand—shine! Keep open house; be generous with your lives. By opening up to others, you'll prompt people to open up with God, this generous Father in heaven. (Matthew 5:14-16 MSG)

Notice the connections here to the self-conscious aims of Jesus and our calling to be his cooperative friends:

- Jesus is the light of the world (John 8:12)—"I make you light-bearers." (Matthew 5:14 MSG)
- Jesus pitched his tent and, moving into the neighborhood, lived among us (see John 1 MSG)—"I'm putting you on a light stand. . . . Shine!" (Matthew 5:15 MSG)
- Jesus spent time in the homes of fiends and sinners—"Keep open house." (Matthew 5:16 MSG)
- Even when he had little in the way of earthly goods, Jesus practiced generous hospitality toward his disciples—"Be generous with your lives." (Matthew 5:16 MSG)
- Jesus said, "Here I am! I stand at the door and knock. If anyone hears my voice and opens the door, I will come in and eat with that person, and they with me " (Revelation 3:20)—"Open up to others." (Matthew 5:15 MSG)

## TABLE FELLOWSHIP WITH SINNERS

*Sent-ness* implies *to-ness*: sent *to* what, *to* whom? The answer is that the church is sent to the places of brokenness, pain, sin, and injustice in the world to be God's agents of healing, justice, and redemption. This work can and does occur in variety of settings, but table fellowship is where light and darkness often came together in the life of Jesus.

In Jesus' day sharing a table and meal with someone was an occurrence that made a bold statement about *withness*, about solidarity. And there were strict rules about with whom one could eat. For instance, "since Gentiles were unclean and uncleanness was contagious, Jews were not to eat with them. [And] the rule applied by Jews to Gentiles was also applied by the religious to the irreligious within Judaism."[2] Jesus created space to be with outcasts in generous, open-hearted ways. Sadly, his way of life and ministry was scandalous to those who practiced bad religion.

Thus, when Jesus ate with people who were obviously sinners, or nonreligious, or not respectable, or part of a Jewish sect it was in vogue to hate, or a Samaritan, it made one of two statements, depending on one's point of view. If one was inclined to reject Jesus, as were the religious leaders of the day, wrong table fellowship said that Jesus was an errant Jew, not a valid rabbi and certainly not the holy Messiah. But from another point of view, it shouted one of the central aims of God in Jesus: God had returned to Zion, to his people! God is with us—all of us, those near to his purposes for them, and those far off. God is doing as he promised: returning to us and calling us to him from the four corners of the world. He is sitting at table with us! It seems that "for Jesus it was communion first, conversion second."[3]

To get an imagination for how Jesus interacted with outsiders and called them to be with him, we must see that "Jesus lived in the world and freely associated with all, unconstrained by the purity prescriptions [of his day]."[4] Jesus "ate with sinners and kept company with people normally on or beyond the borders of respectable society—which of course in his day and culture, meant not merely social responsibility, but religious uprightness, proper covenant behavior, loyalty to the traditions, and hence to the aspirations of Israel."[5]

This was as radical as it sounds. Jesus demonstrated love, grace, mercy, and inclusion toward people with whom it was thought a good Jew—much more the Messiah—should have nothing to do with. But the contrary is true: in the table fellowship of Jesus, we see who indeed is loved and called by God. We get a picture of who is blessed. We recognize those for whom the doors of the kingdom are thrown wide open.

Ben Meyer is especially helpful regarding the various effects of Jesus' table fellowship with sinners: "Nothing, it would seem, had been so overlooked and unexpected as God's boundless goodness toward the simple, the afflicted, and the outcasts; accordingly, nothing in Jesus's career was so thoroughly misconstrued and resented as the resolute, unabashed, symbol-charged dealing with them. What appears in Christian retrospect as a compelling epiphany of love appeared in the swift and unrepeatable drama of history as a contemptuous trampling of tradition."[6]

Jesus was anything but an institutionalist. Why? Did he have a bad attitude? Had he, like many of us, been disappointed or hurt or abused by religious institutions? No; none of those. In Jesus' case, it was this: his love and acceptance could not be bound by, but rather needed to transcend any existing social, re- ligious, or political norms. Popular religious and social norms could not be allowed to restrict God's work in and through Jesus.

Thoughtful observation of Jesus' table fellowship with a noto- rious tax collector, Zacchaeus, led Luke to assert about Jesus, "The Son of Man came to seek and save the lost" (Luke 19:10). Thinking of the three parables in Luke 15 (the lost coin, sheep, and son), Jesus is the kind of Messiah who would move every- thing in the house to find a missing person. He is the kind of shepherd who always seeks the lost sheep. He is the kind of father who longs for wayward daughters and sons to come home—and feasts with them when they do.

We are to get in on this hospitable love, first as recipients and then as those who pass it on. "In the end, this is what love longs to be: capable of meaningful action in the life of the beloved, so committed to the beloved that everything meaningful is at risk. If we want flourishing, this is what we will have to learn."[7]

Two insights from Tom Wright give us further imagination for this:

"God intends to put the world to rights; he has dramatically launched this project through Jesus. Those who belong to Jesus are called, here and now, in the power of the Spirit, to be agents of that putting-to-rights purpose."[8]

"The church is never more in danger than when it sees itself simply as the solution-bearer and forgets that every day it too must say, 'Lord, have mercy on me, a sinner,' and allow that confession to work its way into genuine humility even as it stands boldly before the world and its crazy empires."[9]

Humility and justice-in-action are two key ingredients of good religion. Thus, core to discipleship in Jesus is the transformation of the misaligned aspects of our life so that we can stop living sinfully and cooperate with Jesus in the divine intention to defeat evil and the suffering it produces.

## I WANT IN ON IT

Tom Wright has said that "the call of the gospel is for the church to implement the victory of God in the world through suffering love."[10] To get in on that calling, there is one crucial, decisive thing we need. We must hold true in our deepest being a conviction of something that goes beyond Bible verses or even technically precise Christology. We need to embrace in heart and mind that Jesus is the greatest, truest, most capable, wisest, utmost in demonstrating virtuous love, and the most God-centered person in human history. As the Messiah of the world, sent by God, he was also humanity, Israel, and the church as God intended. To get in on Jesus' model of religion we must think him so wise, so intelligent, and so full of insight that we would naturally and joyfully give credence to him and follow him.

In one of Paul's letters to the Corinthians we see a classic model of someone trying to live into their calling in alignment with the aims of Jesus and to do so for the sake of others. Paul constantly had to defend his motives and goals, his apostleship and ministry among the Corinthians:

> Even though I am free of the demands and expectations of everyone, I have voluntarily become a servant to any and all in order to reach a wide range of people: religious, nonreligious, meticulous moralists, loose-living immoralists, the defeated, the demoralized—whoever. I didn't take on their way of life. I kept my bearings in Christ—but I entered their world and tried to experience things from their point of view. I've become just about every sort of servant there is in my attempts to lead those I meet into a God-saved life. I did all this because of the Message. I didn't just want to talk about it; I wanted to be in on it! (1 Corinthians 9:19-23 MSG)

In this paragraph I observe several characteristics that enable Paul's clear desire to live in alignment with the aims of Jesus.

Why was Paul free from the demands and expectations of others? Because he had given himself to his calling and to fulfilling the expectations of God. This is true freedom and authentic human flourishing.

What did he do with his freedom? He voluntarily became a servant to any sort of person in his life—he started where they were, not where he might have wished they were. This is deep personal security on display.

Where did he get this sense of security? As the natural response to his calling, cooperating with the Spirit's work within him, he cultivated the life and aims of Jesus within himself.

What kept Paul focused and straight? What was the quality of being from which came these core values? "I entered their world and tried to experience things from their point of view . . . [but] I didn't take on their way of life. I kept my bearings in Christ" (1 Corinthians 9:21). He had a vision of what life and ministry should and could be. He knew that Jesus interacted with all manner of people and stayed true to God.

Jesus once explained this himself, "I'm telling you this straight. The Son can't independently do a thing, only what he sees the Father doing. What the Father does, the Son does. The Father loves the Son and includes him in everything he is doing" (John 5:19-20 MSG). The relational reliance Jesus modeled with his Father is mimicked between Paul and Spirit. This is how Paul never lost his bearings.

Why did Paul pursue such a life? He wanted to be in on what God was doing in and through Jesus. This reveals a simple, but decisive structure of desire: Paul aimed at what Jesus did. Paul's true heart was on display as he wrote to his churches, "I want to know Christ . . . becoming like him" (Philippians 3:10); "I have been crucified with Christ and I no longer live, but Christ lives in me. The life I now live in the body, I live by faith in the Son of God, who loved me and gave himself for me" (Galatians 2:20).

Those are lovely, warm, humble, and passionate responses to one's calling. They demonstrate someone rightly grasping and diligently pursuing the aims of Jesus. They are the path to life in alignment with God's intention for humanity.

## THE DESIRE FOR SIGNIFICANCE

We want our life to have meaning. Church leaders want to make a difference in the world. We talk a lot about making an impact on our city, nation, or world. In its place, when not motivated by ego or churned up by narcissism, when kept in sync with other responsibilities in life, this is fine. The search for significance is hardwired by God into the human condition. We were made to count for good.

Paul taught it this way: "We are God's handiwork, created in Christ Jesus to do good works, which God prepared in advance for us to do" (Ephesians 2:10). This means that all of us are "never-ceasing spiritual beings with a unique eternal calling to count for good in God's great universe."[11] Jesus came among us, with his unique aims, to model for us how to live such a life. As he followed his Father, we, through the person and work of the Holy Spirit, are meant to learn from Jesus how to live in alignment with and express his aims. This is what Jesus and I (and you) are meant to be doing together. It is how we are a part of Jesus' ongoing life on earth.

I have learned that as I act in harmony and rhythm with the aims of Jesus, God acts with me and we are then cooperative friends, enjoying the relationship he intended for humanity. God has "framed our nature to function in a conscious, personal relationship of interactive responsibility . . . in union with God, as he acts with us . . . as our constant companion . . . in the creative enterprise of life on earth."[12]

To be healthy, this search for significance must be directed outward. In seeking to align our lives to the aims of Jesus we don't merely seek personal piety. We always seek to act with God in Christ for the healing, redemption, and full flourishing of all persons and the whole of creation. I've had decades now to think about all this and my testimony is this: living into the life God designed for me fulfills the deepest longings of my heart. I go awry and become frustratingly empty when I seek anything else.

God's life—as revealed in and through Jesus, and announced in Jesus' gospel, and observed in his aims—is the true home of the human soul. Any other desire, want, or aim will leave us wanting more. Jesus was not just spouting empty religious jargon when he said, "Everyone who drinks this water [normal water from a well—signifying the fulfillment of earthly pursuits] will be thirsty again, but whoever drinks the water I give them will never thirst. Indeed, the water I give them will become in them a spring of water welling up to eternal life" (John 4:13-14).

We can enter this realm of deep human fulfillment by simply placing our confidence in Jesus, becoming his friend, and following him, placing our trust in the kingdom-gospel announced by Jesus, hearing his call, and taking on his aims. The great promise of God and great gift to us is that in doing so we will be renewed from the depths of our souls—and *the others* in our lives will begin to experience our spirituality as for their good.

## SENT INTO A GOD-BATHED WORLD

Jesus' world and the religious scene of his day, in its own specific ways, was as messed up as ours. That being the case, what do we imagine Jesus experienced when things went wrong, when injustice and evil won in a given moment? Since the Scriptures do not always speak plainly about what Jesus thought or felt, it is a risk to read between the lines. However, based on the totality of the scriptural portrayal of the relationship between Jesus and the Father, we can say this: bad things never drove the good God from Jesus' heart or consciousness. This is what is crucial for those of us who are wearied to despair about the goings-on in the world and the state of the church: The broken world and flawed church are places where God still dwells. He is not driven away by that which is broken and flawed. Instead, those places are the context for his healing, restorative love.

The world as we know it came from God. Despite its sinful brokenness, God has never abandoned it. God is never in denial about what is real, but he sees creation through a lens that includes the perfections that he himself designed and spoke into being. God does not just see the million pieces of busted up pottery, he sees the invaluable vase. He does not merely observe the addict, the fear-driven, the sexually confused, the rebellious, the wasteful consumption, the racism, classism, the gender inequities—God sees his intention for humanity. We are always before his eyes and cherished in his heart. Our brokenness does not give God amnesia or make him blind. He is a realist and takes it all in. But he does so in way that the joy of his creative impulse remains.

Jesus operated from the experiential knowledge of this God-bathed world. Such firsthand knowledge banishes fear, even the despairing conviction "that nothing ever changes," or that "I try my best but fail to change things—bad things keep happening in the world, in the church, and in my life."

Regret and grieving are a normal and frequent aspect of Christian spirituality. While they are real, they are not ultimate or determinative. Rather, normative to life in God's kingdom is the experience of being cherished by him, feeling his never-ceasing presence, hearing his calling to take our life up into his and to become his cooperative friends. Within himself, and from his self-sustaining being, God is continuously fresh in wise love and right-directed power. Life in him—like a branch to a vine (John 15:1-8)—is our hope and remedy for the moments we feel bankrupt regarding faith, hope, peace, and love.

We cannot move out in faith based on a God who we believe is as depressed and powerless as we sometimes feel. Why would we even believe in such a God, much less worship him, or act as his cooperative friend? We wouldn't and couldn't—and we don't. This is what makes the gift of perspective, of insight, so vital. If we have seen Jesus, in his boundless joy standing between his Father and a misaligned Israel, an evil world, and a set of new disciples who barely get what he is up to, we have both seen the Father and the way the Father enables us, in Christ, by the Spirit, to be present to our world.

Dallas Willard reveals the spiritual trajectory of being in the world in the way of Jesus: The heavens are progressively open to us as our character and understanding are increasingly attuned to the realities of God's rule from the heavens.[13] As our spirit opens to this reality, we come to know that a totally good and competent God is right here with us to look after us.[14]

Being *looked after* is the rocket fuel for *looking after* others in love, joy, and peace. Such knowledge is meant to be the home for our soul and the safe launching pad from which we join with God in his cosmic endeavor to overthrow the evil that seems so dominant in our world and to renew his creation all-inclusively through his originative, insistent, powerful love.

That is the distant echo that reverberates in my heart when despair over the church grips my life. It sometimes feels harder and harder to hear; yet I, like you, desire to be an agent of good in the world. It is an effort to make our way through the debris of religious hurts, to find our way back to Jesus, to discipleship in Jesus for the good of others.

## A MODEL CHURCH

When I am asked to cite a church and its leaders that did an especially good job implementing the aims of Jesus, I always name Gordon Cosby and Elizabeth O'Connor, leaders of Church of the Savior, two miles north of the White House, in the Adams Morgan district of Washington, DC.

In their work, they modeled the aims of Jesus in what they called the journey inward of spiritual transformation into Christlikeness, and the journey outward,[15] in which members learned that co-creation as cooperative friends of God is the essence of what it means to be human. The journeys inward and outward go together, forming a mutuality that shapes in us good religion. There are aspects of our inner life, our heart and soul, that will never be transformed until we take the risk of serving others.

While serving others, we will come to notice our lack of love, spiritual power, faith, and hope. This recognition will drive us back to the inward journey. And then round and round we go, ever growing in Jesus.

Through frequent silent retreats as well as the cultivation of a daily life attentive to God, Church of the Savior called their congregation to abandon habits of abusive, narcissistic leadership. They gave vision for the church to forsake structures of bad religion in favor of servant structures that released Spirit-empowered work through lay people. They shaped a freeing organization in which the practices of good religion could be held gently.[16] They led Church of the Savior to commit to the aims of Jesus.[17] They taught their congregation to discern how God might be calling them to use their gifts.[18]

In their prime years they were a community of stunning creativity yielding copious acts of good religion. Helping members find their truest selves in the service of others, they became shepherds to the homeless, advocates for the poor, healers of the drug addicted, and safe places for abused women.

I've never known a church that better married gentleness with true Spirit empowerment, that better paired humility with confident faith, that were gathered as a loving, supportive, healing community while simultaneously being sent by God into their neighborhood as ambassadors of good religion.

They encourage me every time I remember them. What we dream is possible. Good religion is attainable. I've seen it in at least one truly great church.

### EXERCISE
### APPLYING THE AIMS OF JESUS TO MY LIFE

1. Recall a time in your life when you were using the gifts the Spirit gave you. How did they give shape and capacity for a calling? If thinking about this evokes memories that seem

like the distant past, I invite you to inquire of God what it might look and feel like for those gifts to return.

2. What are a couple of the harmful experiences in the church that other people have shared with you? How have other's experiences impaired your ability to enter into a healing conversation with God? Are you inadvertently stacking up negatives about church and failing to see the good? Just be honestly aware and talk to God about it.

3. With whom can you have redemptive table fellowship? Is there a Zacchaeus in your social sphere? Think of someone who you would delight to be with and have a meaningful spiritual conversation—then ask to meet them or have them over for a meal.

---

You might begin with this prayer:

*God, I miss the innocence of my first love for you, for others, and for the church. I long for the simple days when I heard your voice with innocence and followed it, when I heard your calling and knew that you and I were working together to bless others. Please stir up my gifts. Let me hear your calling again. Send me into the world with love and your capacity to do the good you envision me to do.*

What words of your own would you like to add?

# 11

# DO MY RELIGIOUS RESERVATIONS AND CHURCHLY HESITATIONS DISQUALIFY ME?

## JESUS WALKS WITH US ON A JOURNEY OF DOUBT

*These are written that you may believe that Jesus is the Messiah, the Son of God, and that by believing you may have life in his name.*

**JOHN 20:31**

*We would like to meet Jesus.*

**JOHN 12:21 CEV**

*Don't be afraid; just believe.*

**MARK 5:36**

*Come, follow me.*

**MARK 1:17**

**The date had been on my calendar** for many months, and I was looking forward to the evening. Like someone on the first day of a new job, I was keen to get to my office early to set up tables and chairs suitable for hosting a conversation, get the coffee brewed, heat water for tea, put some water bottles on ice, and lay the packaged snacks out in a hospitable way. Surveying the room and being satisfied with its vibe, I sat down to await my guests. My anticipation was high because since my earliest days as a teenage convert, I have been fascinated by how the mix of faith and doubt work within human beings.

To do some basic-level research on the contemporary state of faith and doubt, I hosted a few conversations that were advertised in church announcements as *Issues of Faith*. Anyone could come, members of the church, or friends or family who were dechurched. One by one participants arrived, greeted each other, got whatever they wanted to drink or snack on, and sat down around a table.

As an introduction for the evening, I reminded the group of our purpose for coming together: to discover today's real issues of faith—those that individuals in the group have and those which, in their observation, seem common in others. With a bit of opening discussion, it was easy to get the group focused on why we were having the conversation: that a core aspect of following Jesus is to discover and fearlessly name whatever it is in our actual beliefs about God (not what we think we should or ought to believe) that makes confidence in Jesus seem hard or impractical.

I did not have to do much to keep the conversation going. Ideas poured out until I had to halt the group at our agreed-on stopping time. Highlights from my notes include these issues of faith:

Bill revealed that he did not know exactly what to think about human sexuality, that everyone seems to have a different take on it. "But," he said, "I do know one thing: I don't like the hateful rhetoric around the topic. I want to know how to be biblically orthodox (assuming we can figure *truth* out!) and loving at the same time. How do I discern if I am just bending to society, or being enlightened and more caring, or waffling on an important biblical issue?"

Sam revealed that he was afraid that having any clear view of morality derived from the Bible would make him seem like a bigot, an ignorant hater, or a worse sort of human being. He wondered, "If I insist on Christianity being the only right way, isn't that elitist, judgmental, and proud?" He said lots of people he knows think religion is not just wrong, but harmful. From the Crusades to present forms of religious terrorism, religion seems bent on the destruction of others. It is a big source of malevolence in the world.

Marty said he and many people he knows cannot understand how prayer works, why so much suffering in the world continues despite many fervent prayers that it would cease. He wondered why the Scripture says, "I give you bread, not a stone," but so often it seems that God in fact gives us "stones." "I invested in my kid," Marty said. "I did all the right Bible and churchly things, but he is still an addict and continues in his destructive behavior. Watching my son, whom I love so much, destroy his life and harm others along the way erodes my trust in God. Friends and family say they see this and wonder why they should consider God when it doesn't seem to work for me, for that which I care about most." Marty struggled to hold back tears as he said, "I am tired of hearing that 'God has a plan for your life.' The promise that some magnificent life change is coming feels like a carrot that one can never quite grasp, a mirage in the distance that never becomes water to truly quench my spiritual thirst."

Doubt and skepticism are real. In many cases they are understandable. We might even say that they are a part of faith development, the raw material from which genuine confidence in God is created. As Frederick Buechner memorably put it, "Without somehow destroying me in the process, how could God reveal himself in a way that would leave no room for doubt? If there were no room for doubt, there would be no room for me."[1]

But we must grapple with this: Jesus never commended doubt as a settled state. He never said, "Blessed is your honest cynicism, for it has made you whole," or "Happy are those who are full of skepticism, for they shall see the kingdom of God." Jesus put a premium on faith and the obedient actions that flow from it.

Nevertheless, lots of people do have reservations about faith. They are skeptical about religious dogma. They have become cynical about all religion and hopeless regarding things at church. That is the reality.

What now? How does one move forward when doubt pushes against budding faith, when uncertainty works to shrink what little religious confidence one may have? The first idea is to know that Jesus is patient with those who are struggling with faith. His first friends experienced his easygoing lovingkindness, and their writings help us to have confidence in the gracious love of Jesus.

## TRUSTING THE TESTIMONY OF GOD

As we've worked together, this much has become clear: Jesus was not a wandering wonderer. He knew things. He grasped reality like no other human being before or after him. This means he was not a drifter, flitting though life spouting nonsense. Rather, he specifically and carefully directed his words and deeds to the accomplishing of his aims.

He once said, "The prince of this world is coming. He has no hold over me" (John 14:30). That is complete renunciation and separation from any worldly aim. Jesus further said, "I have come down from heaven not to do my will but to do the will of him who sent me" (John 6:38) and, "My food . . . is to do the will of him who sent me and to finish his work" (John 4:34). That is complete identification with his Father, with his Father's kingdom aims.

The Gospel writer, John, was Jesus' best friend. He passionately wanted others to know Jesus and to take on Christlikeness.

Citing some logic that would help his readers move in that direction, he wrote,

> If we take human testimony at face value, how much more should we be reassured when God gives testimony as he does here, testifying concerning his Son. Whoever believes in the Son of God inwardly confirms God's testimony. Whoever refuses to believe in effect calls God a liar, refusing to believe God's own testimony regarding his Son. (1 John 5:9-10 MSG)

God has most boldly, precisely, and clearly made himself and his intentions known in the person and work of Jesus. If you ask, "Where now is some semblance of truth, source authority, or coherence for life?" start with what God spoke publicly about his Son during two vital events of Jesus' life.

At Jesus' baptism, he was coming up out of the water, and "at that moment heaven was opened . . . and a voice from heaven said, 'This is my Son, whom I love; with him I am well pleased'" (Matthew 3:13-17). And at the transfiguration, "a bright cloud covered [everyone there], and a voice from the cloud said, 'This is my Son, whom I love; with him I am well pleased. Listen to him!'" (Matthew 17:5).

Perhaps Jesus was reflecting on those moments when he said, "The Father who sent me bears witness about me" (John 8:18 ESV). Jesus certainly was deeply conscious of what his Father was doing in and through him, and he often mentioned it.

You may recall a time, when having been hurt by a nasty rumor or destructive criticism, a loving person advised you to consider the source. Those words are normally meant to point to us a corrupt motivation or a critic's inability to know the truth of things. Let's put a positive twist on "consider the source" and see if you can agree with me on something important: ancient people were at least as intelligent and moral as you or me. They were able to represent reality to others in honest, reliable words suitable to their era. They may not have had Facebook as a tool for communication or possessed an understanding of social media algorithms, but they knew how to describe their experiences accurately and honestly.

This was never truer than in their ability to articulate their familiarity with Jesus. A representative moment is captured in Matthew 9:35-36:

> Jesus went through all the towns and villages, teaching in their synagogues proclaiming the good news of the kingdom and healing every disease and sickness. When he saw the crowds, he had compassion on them, because they were harassed and helpless, like sheep without a shepherd.

Among normal people, the ancient testimony concerning Jesus highlighted his authoritative wisdom about the inbreaking of the kingdom of God. Compassion was a standout feature of Jesus' ministry. Crowds said, "No one ever spoke the way this man does" (John 7:46). His explanations of reality led people to hear him gladly, to be astonished at his insight, and to marvel at his thinking, saying things like, "We have never heard anyone teach with such authority!" (see Matthew 7:28-29). Jesus' insights were full-orbed wisdom for the full-orbed needs of humanity. It was his obvious, experienced wisdom that gave Jesus authority with crowds. For those who believed him, those reliable, respected insights bound them tightly to Jesus.

## THE AIMS OF JESUS' TEACHING

What was the burden of Jesus' teaching? Did it have any center of gravity and controlling perspective, or was it a somewhat random collection of wise fables and religious sayings? What expressed and unexpressed presuppositions undergirded his teaching? What made Jesus' teaching meaningful and coherent?

Jesus was calling for "a disposition conditioning the whole conduct of life . . . [marked by an] appetite for the will of God—as the act of accepting his reign."[2] The teaching of Jesus emerged from a matchless inner dynamism and spirit. Reaching backward and forward at the same time, it made sense of Israel's troubled past and articulated its promised future.

Recalling Jesus' clarifying pronouncement, "Do not think that I have come to abolish the Law or the Prophets; I have not come to abolish them but to fulfill them" (Matthew 5:17), we are able to grasp that "Jesus' aim is to mediate the final, climactic revelation of God's will, thus bringing the teaching of Torah and prophets to its full, divinely predetermined, eschatological measure of completeness."[3]

Jesus was "the proclaimer of God's kingdom initiative—and all his teaching traits [and healing, delivering actions] were in service to this."[4] As the Second Person of the Trinity, Jesus taught in a very different voice and vitality than the other religious leaders of his day; "his authority was *personal* not exegetical."[5] His focused teaching about the kingdom of God was the basis for his call to conversion. He proclaimed the reign of God to "summon the sons [and daughters] of that reign."[6]

Jesus is patient with our journey, but there cannot be a journey without a path—and Jesus was not shy about pointing to, modeling, and calling people to one way in and through him. "The *commands* of Jesus were the heart of his teaching and reflected the revolutionary significance of the reign of God and specified the right response to it."[7]

For instance, Jesus said,

- "Why do you call me, 'Lord, Lord,' and do not do what I say?" (Luke 6:46)
- "Whoever wants to be my disciple must deny themselves and take up their cross and follow me. For whoever wants to

save their life will lose it, but whoever loses their life for me and for the gospel will save it." (Mark 8:34-35)

- "No one who puts a hand to the plow and looks back is fit for service in the kingdom of God." (Luke 9:62)
- "Whoever disowns me before others, I will disown before my Father in heaven." (Matthew 10:33)
- "Go in through the narrow gate. The gate to destruction is wide, and the road that leads there is easy to follow. A lot of people go through that gate." (Matthew 7:13 CEV)
- "Go out quickly into the streets and alleys of the town and bring in the poor, the crippled, the blind and the lame. . . . Go out to the roads and country lanes and compel them to come in, so that my house will be full. I tell you, not one of those who [declined my invitation] will get a taste of my banquet." (Luke 14:21-24)
- "Whoever wants to be my disciple must deny themselves and take up their cross daily and follow me." (Luke 9:23)
- "My mother and brothers are those who hear God's word and put it into practice." (Luke 8:21)

The grace-saturated invitation to follow Jesus is the greatest offer any of us will ever receive.

One cannot hear Jesus without reacting in some way. Some might try to do away with Jesus as his contemporaries did (Mark 11:18; 12:12; Luke 11:53; 22:2). Another might be amazed at the authority of his teaching and become convinced by it (John 7:17). One could also remain lukewarm—which might be the worst state of all (Revelation 3:16). It is always true: the teaching of Jesus compels his hearers to make a decision.

God's life as revealed in and through Jesus, announced in Jesus' gospel, and observed in his aims, is the true home of the human soul. Any other desire, want, or aim will leave us wanting more. Jesus was not just spouting empty words when he said,

"Everyone who drinks this water will be thirsty again, but whoever drinks the water I give them will never thirst. Indeed, the water I give them will become in them a spring of water welling up to eternal life" (John 4:13-14).

We can enter this realm of deep human fulfillment by simply placing our confidence in Jesus, becoming his friend, and following him; by placing our confidence in his gospel (the kingdom of God); by hearing his call and taking on his aims. The great promise of God and the great gift of God to us is that in following Jesus, we will be renewed from the depths of our souls, and the others in our life will experience us, and our religiousness, as for their good.

Jesus' perspective that the world was saturated with such a God, and that bad religion was an impostor, was not an exercise in denial. We know this by simply recalling the number of times he called out bad religion and healed the effects of it. This idea is core to our work in this book: *One of the foremost aims of Jesus is to heal the evil of bad religion and the despair we feel in the face of the human atrocities that invade our personal lives and bombard our news feeds. Jesus aims to breathe new life into our desire to follow him and to be agents of God's good purposes in the world.*

## A PLACE TO JOURNEY IN THE CHURCH

Creating a Christ-centered, childlike, light, and easy space to explore faith is both the vision and the atmosphere of Journey Church in Franklin, Tennessee. Two of their pastors, Suzie Lind and Kevin Dixon are new friends who I have come to know through justice initiatives in which we all work. I've had a couple meetings at their church, and as Suzie walked me around the building, introducing herself and telling me the story of the church, I came to highly respect Journey's approach with those who are struggling with issues of faith.

Journey Church is not a prototypical seeker church, but they have always been oriented toward the spiritually open and curious. Given their Nashville-area location, that meant they created spaces in which the artistic and musical communities of Nashville, with their unique creativity and worldview, felt welcome. It surprised Journey when they also became a church for another outlier group: bikers. These two groups are icons of an overall vibe that makes people welcome regardless of the maturity of their faith or lack of it.

Interviewing Suzie, I asked, "How has Journey made space for people who are skeptical of church to make their way toward faith?"

Suzie replied without hesitation and with joy: "We welcome questions. We are very comfortable with people not knowing everything and with them questioning things they think they might know. We never want people to feel shame for having sincere questions about faith." Space for searching and a welcome of curiosity are the lovely and difference-making spices of Journey Church.

As Suzie was talking, and I was trying to keep up taking notes, a line from a poem kept distracting me, calling for my attention:

Be patient toward all that is unsolved in your heart

and try to love the questions themselves. . . .

It is a matter of living everything. Live the questions now.[8]

Something rings humanly true in these words by Rainer Maria Rilke, maybe most especially concerning the mystery of faith: we will either come to love questions and value them as pointers or steppingstones to faith or we will pretend, become hypocrites, judge others, and engage in self-condemnation.

Four of Jesus' best friends—Peter, James, John, and Judas—all had wrong ideas about him, but Jesus never gave up on them. He walked with them, revealed himself to them, loved them, washed their feet, and gave them Communion. Jesus is comfortable with honest questions. Journey Church creates a Jesus space. At Journey there is no judgment and no expectation to be something you are not.

I asked Suzie what they have learned over the years, and I especially valued an anecdote she shared: There are two ways to keep cattle. One, build fences; two, dig a well. As she was talking, I immediately thought of social set theory.[9] "Yes," she said, "that is right. This is a pictorial way to describe bounded set (the fence) and center set (the well) realities." She went on to say that Journey could decide to build fences that clearly keep the right people in and the wrong people out—and feel smugly good about it. But Journey decided to dig a powerfully flowing well of healing water called Jesus and to then encourage seekers to stay close to the water source, to orient their life toward the well, moving toward it, never wandering away from it.

Suzie told me these two core values—honor questions and show people how to stay close to Jesus with their questions—are deeply appreciated by those who are exhausted by pretending they have all the answers, and who reject judgmental fences. They simply don't want to be a part of churches like that anymore. They tell Suzie and the church staff that Journey is their last stop before giving up on church.

Because they see the image of God in everyone, there is no place for shame in the life of Journey Church. Shame is never used as a tool to bring about obedience. There is conviction regarding amendment of belief and lifestyle, but the specific changes and their pace come from the Holy Spirit.

A final insight from Suzie sticks with me. She said that, in her observation, "I've given up on the church, but not Jesus" does not work for long. Over time, outside a community that supports a questioning journey to faith, Jesus will indeed recede from our focus too.

Struggling wanderers seeking faith love Journey Church and the hospitable, generous vibe in which they can be real on their way to life devoted to Jesus. Journey is a great church because they have done two things: (1) they have stayed passionately focused on Jesus, and (2) they have created a faith community that mirrors Jesus' loving patience for pilgrims who, traversing the rugged terrain of doubt and confusion, are provided a safe watering hole for their journey to faith.

## RESCUING JESUS' REPUTATION TO SAVE MY SOUL

Over these pages we've heard stories of bad religion in the words of real people. We've looked at the aims of Jesus and discovered that they are the basis of true, good religion. We've seen examples of noble religion in churches and followers of Jesus seeking to live in alignment with his aims.

Finishing a draft of this book while on sabbatical, the quiet of that sabbath rest brought a reality to the surface: I needed to rescue the reputation of Jesus for myself. Only the Jesus we have been contemplating can save my—our—soul. I sincerely empathize with those who are done with church. I can say along with the great thinker Howard Thurman, "For years it has been a part of my own quest so to understand the religion of Jesus that interest in his way of life could be developed and sustained by intelligent men and women who were at the same time deeply victimized by the Christian Church's betrayal of his faith."[10]

It surprises most of us, but *alignment* to Jesus results in *abundance* of life.

There is reliable medicine for curing the abuse of bad religion. There is a focus of, source of, and sure path to good religion: "Fixing our eyes on Jesus, the pioneer and perfecter of faith" (Hebrews 12:2).

Study how he did it. Because he never lost sight of where he was headed—that exhilarating finish in and with God—he could put up with anything along the way: cross, shame, whatever.

And now he's there, in the place of honor, right alongside God. "When you find yourselves flagging in your faith, go over that story again, item by item, that long litany of hostility he plowed through. *That* will shoot adrenaline into your souls!" (Hebrews 12:2-3 MSG).

## APPLYING THE AIMS OF JESUS TO MY LIFE

1. Having come this far with me, check in with your heart. Where are you now? How have your heart issues shifted as you've read? What encouragement or healing you can name, and for what can you give thanks to God?

2. What do you find encouraging about the story of Journey Church? Have you encountered a church like Journey that is open to questions and those dealing with bad religion? If so, express your thanks to God. If not, name any desire, longing, and sadness.

3. If you are moved by the story of churches like Journey maybe you are called by God to be a person of spiritual hospitality, who creates safe spaces in which people can be on their journey regarding faith. How might you create hospitable spaces in your context to provide good care for people to bring their doubts, questions, and harmful experiences with the church?

You might begin with this prayer:

*God, you know I have been all over the map in my faith journey. I have felt anxious, angry, and confused. One minute I relentlessly shame myself for not being able to get it together and the next minute I blame the church for everything. Thank you that you have been patient with me throughout this journey. Thank you that you never leave me or cast me out. I am following behind you, Lord, but I am walking with a limp.*

What words of your own would you like to add?

# ACKNOWLEDGMENTS

**I first saw the expression** "the aims of Jesus" twenty years ago in Bishop N. T. (Tom) Wright's *Jesus and the Victory of God*. I recall thinking, *Aims, plural? What the heck is Tom talking about? Didn't Jesus, as I had been taught, merely come to die for our sins?* Later, hearing of my enthusiasm for Tom's work, my friend and colleague Scot McKnight introduced me to Ben F. Meyer's book *The Aims of Jesus.*

This book has its origin, energy, and flow in the scholarly, original thinking of Wright and Meyer. Their work on the aims of Jesus has flowed through my life, deepening my desire, and focusing my intent to be a constant, consistent, whole-life follower of Jesus—seeking to align my heart, soul, mind, emotions, will, and social relations with his aims.

I am grateful for the team at IVP. They hung in with me over a period of years as we tried to chisel a book from the rock of my ideas about how the aims of Jesus might re-present him and gain a fresh hearing for him among those struggling with religion and church. Beginning with our first project more than ten years ago, Cindy Bunch, now associate publisher at IVP, has been a consistent source of serene patience. She is more than an editor to me. She is a friend whom I trust wholeheartedly. In many ways, she has given me confidence to write and mentored me along the way. Her team shares her vision and vibe. Ethan McCarthy gave me difference-making constructive criticism on the first draft. Rachel Hastings inspired me with the idea and sparked the courage in me to tell some of my story for the sake of my readers.

Tianna Haas's guidance enhanced the coherence and flow of the book.

When I was stuck, trying to get my ideas clear for articulating the aims of Jesus, Cindy introduced me to Margot Starbuck. Margot is a multitalented woman—writer, editor, communicator, and coach. She inspires me to be an ever-greater servant to my readers.

My friend Suzie Lind, executive pastor of ministries at Journey Church in Franklin, Tennessee, read early chapters and gave encouraging feedback.

My colleague at the Center for Formation, Justice and Peace, Vanessa Sadler, a trauma-trained spiritual director, worked with me on the exercises, refining them with her love and wisdom.

I am honored to have Esau McCaulley write the foreword to this book. I have high regard for Esau as a talented colleague and treasure him as a trusted friend.

# NOTES

### INTRODUCTION

[1] Jeffrey M. Jones, "Confidence in U.S. Institutions Down; Average at New Low," Gallup, July 5, 2022, https://news.gallup.com/poll/394283/confidence-institutions-down-average-new-low.aspx.

[2] Frank Newport, "Fewer in U.S. Now See Bible as Literal Word of God," Gallup, July 6, 2022, https://news.gallup.com/poll/394262/fewer-bible-literal-word-god.aspx.

[3] Justin Giboney, "Christian Virtue Strengthens the Social Justice Cause," The Public Square, *Christianity Today*, August 24, 2021, www.christianitytoday.com/ct/2021/august-web-only/racism-social-justice-christian-virtue-strengthens.html.

### 1. AM I THE ONLY ONE WHO THINKS THIS?

[1] Jonathan Poletti, "Top 10 Evangelical Sex Scandals of 2021," *Medium*, January 5, 2022, https://medium.com/belover/top-10-evangelical-sex-scandals-of-2021-946d89760e73.

[2] Mike Stunson, "As Pastor Confesses His Adultery, Woman Says in Church She Was the 16-Year-Old Victim," *Kansas City Star*, September 1, 2022, www.kansascity.com/news/nation-world/national/article261741097.html.

[3] Vanessa Buschschlüter, "La Luz del Mundo Megachurch Leader Jailed for Child Sex Abuse," BBC, June 9, 2022, www.bbc.com/news/world-latin-america-61730756.

[4] Peter Smith and Holly Meyer, "#ChurchToo Revelations Growing, Years after Movement Began," AP News, June 12, 2022, https://apnews.com/article/entertainment-health-baptist-religion-c7c5f62a5737b3aee20ceaa3f99ab603.

[5] Ian Austen, "'Horrible History': Mass Grave of Indigenous Children Report in Canada," *New York Times*, May 28, 2021, updated October 5, 2021, www.nytimes.com/2021/05/28/world/canada/kamloops-mass-grave-residential-schools.html.

[6] Jeanne Whalen, "Russian Orthodox Leader Backs War in Ukraine, Divides Faith," Europe, *Washington Post*, April 18, 2022, https://washingtonpost .com/world/2022/04/18/russian-orthodox-church-ukraine-war; and Jason Horowitz, "The Russian Orthodox Leader at the Core of Putin's Ambitions," *New York Times*, May 21, 2022, www.nytimes.com /2022/05/21/world/europe/kirill-putin-russian-orthodox-church.html.

[7] "How Often Do You Attend Church or Synagogue—At Least Once a Week, Almost Every Week, About Once a Month, Seldom, or Never?," Statista, June 21, 2022, www.statista.com/statistics/245491/church-attendance -of-americans.

[8] Thomas Costello, "18 of the Latest Church Statistics You Should Know in 2022," Reach Right Studios, January 4, 2022, https://reachrightstudios .com/church-statistics-2022/#h-1-the-attendance-vs-engagement-shift.

[9] Yonat Shimron, "Study: Attendance Hemorrhaging at Small and Midsize US Congregations," Religion News Service, October 14, 2021, https:// religionnews.com/2021/10/14/study-attendance-at-small-and-midsize -us-congregations-is-hemorrhaging.

[10] Thomas Curwen, "CRT, Trumpism and Doubt Roil Biola University: Is This the Future of Evangelical Christianity?," *Los Angeles Times*, June 27, 2022, www.latimes.com/california/story/2022-06-10/crt-trumpism-doubt -roil-biola-university.

[11] Curwen, "CRT, Trumpism and Doubt."

[12] Justin McCarthy, "U.S. Confidence in Organized Religion Remains Low," *Politics*, Gallup, July 8, 2019, https://news.gallup.com/poll/259964 /confidence-organized-religion-remains-low.aspx.

[13] Kate Shellnutt, "The Pastors Aren't All Right: 38% Consider Leaving Ministry," Research, *Christianity Today*, November 16, 2021, www.christianity today.com/news/2021/november/pastor-burnout-pandemic-barna consider-leaving-ministry.html.

[14] The Animals, "We Gotta Get Out of This Place," by Barry Mann and Cynthia Weil, *We Gotta Get Out of This Place*, MGM, 1965.

[15] Larry Norman, "If God Is My Father," by Larry Norman, *In Another Land*, Solid Rock Records, 1976.

## 2. CAN I FIND FAITH AGAIN?

[1] See Ben Meyer, *The Aims of Jesus*, Princeton Theological Monograph Series (Eugene, OR: Pickwick Publications, 2002); N. T. Wright, *The New Testament and the People of God*, Christian Origins and the Question of God,

vol. 1 (Minneapolis, MN: Fortress Press, 1992); and *Jesus and the Victory of God*, Christian Origins and the Question of God, vol. 2 (Minneapolis, MN: Fortress Press, 1997). When Wright talks about the aims of Jesus, he uses historical analysis to reveal how Jesus understood his role in the long story of Israel and how Jesus intended to—aimed to—fulfill that story. Wright notes three significant aims of Jesus: Israel's return from exile; the return of Yahweh to Zion, the defeat of evil. I am borrowing from the Meyer/Wright paradigm, using it to extrapolate the aims of Jesus as they emerge from his manner of being, his teaching, and his deeds of power.

### 3. I AM FAILING TO CONNECT TO FAITH AND CHURCH

[1] Paul Baloche, "Open the Eyes of My Heart," by Paul Baloche, *Open the Eyes of My Heart*, Integrity Music, 2000.

[2] Tom Wright's translation; N. T. Wright, *John for Everyone*, Part 1, The New Testament for Everyone (Louisville, KY: Westminster John Knox Press, 2004), 77.

[3] Billy Graham, "The 'I Ams' of Jesus," *Decision: The Evangelical Voice for Today*, January 14, 2008, https://decisionmagazine.com/the-i-ams -of-jesus.

[4] Wright, *John for Everyone*, Part 1, 116.

[5] Wright, *John for Everyone*, Part 1, 152-53.

[6] N. T. Wright, *John for Everyone*, Part 2, The New Testament for Everyone (Louisville, KY: Westminster John Knox Press, 2004), 8.

### 4. I'VE LOST THE RELIGIOUS PLOT LINE

[1] Ben Meyer, *The Aims of Jesus*, Princeton Theological Monograph Series (Eugene, OR: Pickwick Publications, 2002), 110.

[2] Meyer, *The Aims of Jesus*, 175.

[3] Eugene H. Peterson, *The Message: The Bible in Contemporary Language* (Colorado Springs, CO: NavPress, 2005), 1243.

[4] Jon Meacham, *American Gospel: God, the Founding Fathers, and the Making of a Nation* (New York: Random House, 2007), 187.

[5] David J. Bosch, *Believing in the Future: Toward a Missiology of Western Culture*, Christian Mission and Modern Culture (Chicago, IL: Gracewing, 1998), 3.

### 5. I FEEL PAIN, CYNICISM, AND DESPAIR —WHERE IS JESUS?

[1] See, for instance, N. T. Wright, *Evil and the Justice of God* (Downers Grove, IL: InterVarsity Press); C. S. Lewis, *The Problem of Pain* (New York:

HarperOne); Peter Kreeft, *Making Sense Out Of Suffering* (Ann Arbor, MI: Servant Books).

[2] D. A. Carson, Walter W. Wessel, and Walter L. Liefeld, *The Expositor's Bible Commentary, Matthew, Mark, Luke*, vol. 8 (Grand Rapids, MI: Zondervan), 309-10.

[3] Carson, Wessel, and Liefeld, *The Expositor's Bible Commentary*, 312.

[4] Carson, Wessel, and Liefeld, *The Expositor's Bible Commentary*, 317.

[5] N. T. Wright, *Luke for Everyone*, The New Testament for Everyone (Louisville, KY: Westminster John Knox Press, 2004), 210.

[6] Wright, *Luke for Everyone*, 210, 211 (emphasis is Wright's).

[7] Ben Meyer, *The Aims of Jesus*, Princeton Theological Monograph Series (Eugene, OR: Pickwick Publications, 2002), 145.

[8] Meyer, *The Aims of Jesus*, 145

[9] James K. A. Smith, *You Are What You Love: The Spiritual Power of Habit* (Grand Rapids, MI: Brazos Press), xii.

[10] Smith, *You Are What You Love*, 19-20.

[11] Smith, *You Are What You Love*, 85, 99.

[12] Smith, *You Are What You Love*, 21.

[13] Smith, *You Are What You Love*, 85.

[14] Smith, *You Are What You Love*, 19-20.

[15] Eugene H. Peterson, *The Message: The Bible in Contemporary Language* (Colorado Springs, CO: NavPress, 2005), 1532.

## 6. WHAT ABOUT ALL THE BAD THINGS DONE IN GOD'S NAME?

[1] N. T. Wright, *Surprised by Hope: Rethinking Heaven, the Resurrection, and the Mission of the Church* (New York: HarperCollins, 2008), 141.

[2] Wright, *Surprised by Hope*, 182.

[3] This prayer was said in the order of worship in my local church. It is adapted from "The Prayer for Social Justice" that first appeared in *The 1928 Book of Common Prayer* (New York: Oxford University Press, 1973), 44.

[4] Ralph Martin and Peter Davis, eds., *Dictionary of the Later New Testament and Its Developments*, The IVP Bible Dictionary Series (Downers Grove, IL: IVP Academic), 347.

[5] Martin and Davis, *Dictionary of the Later New Testament*, 347.

[6] Joel Green, Jeannine Brown, and Nicholas Perrin, eds., *Dictionary of Jesus and the Gospels* (Downers Grove, IL: IVP Academic, 2013), 380-81.

[7] Green, Brown, and Perrin, *Dictionary of Jesus and the Gospels*, 380.

[8] Dallas Willard, *The Divine Conspiracy: Rediscovering Our Hidden Life in God* (New York: HarperCollins, 2014), 1.

[9] Matthew Maxey, "The Telling of 'The Fuller Story' in Franklin," Franklin, Tennessee, website, February 9, 2022, https://visitfranklin.com/blog/the-telling-of-the-fuller-story-in-franklin/.

[10] "The Fuller Story," City of Franklin, TN, website, www.franklintn.gov/our-city/the-fuller-story.

[11] Maxey, "The Telling of 'The Fuller Story.'"

[12] Anika Exum, "'It's Part of a March to Freedom,' New Colored Troops Statue Result of Years of Work," *The Tennessean*, October 22, 2021, www.tennessean.com/story/news/local/williamson/2021/10/22/fuller-story-weekend-honoring-united-states-colored-troops-statue/6124475001.

[13] Emily R. West, "Daughters of Confederacy Allege Ownership of Franklin Public Square in Court Filing," *The Tennessean*, November 14, 2018, www.tennessean.com/story/news/local/williamson/2018/11/14/franklin-public-square-ownership-daughters-confederacy/1992956002.

## 7. CAN I TRUST THE CHURCH TO BE AN INSTRUMENT OF RESTORATION?

[1] N. T. Wright, *Matthew for Everyone*, Part 2, The New Testament for Everyone (Louisville, KY: Westminster John Knox Press), 100.

[2] D. A. Carson, Walter W. Wessel, and Walter L. Liefeld, *The Expositor's Bible Commentary: Matthew, Mark, Luke*, vol. 8 (Grand Rapids, MI: Zondervan), 480.

[3] Wright, *Matthew for Everyone*, 103.

[4] Wright, *Matthew for Everyone*, 107.

## 8. HOW CAN I FIND VIBRANT FAITH?

[1] Abuse and abusers are a complex and subtle reality that goes beyond that which can be covered in a brief paragraph. If you have been a victim of abuse, please inform the appropriate institutional authorities or law enforcement officers. "Turn the other cheek" or "Matthew 18" or "two or more witnesses" are not reasons that a person abused by someone in power should be made to "turn the other cheek" or "face their abuser." To suggest so is to make Jesus' teachings silly, unwise, even absurd. Most cases of abuse have no witnesses: privacy and secrecy are two realities that enable abusers. If you are looking for guidance or general information about abuse in the church, see Chuck DeGroat, *When*

*Narcissism Comes to Church: Healing Your Community From Emotional and Spiritual Abuse* (Downers Grove, IL: InterVarsity Press, 2020); Scot McKnight and Laura Barringer, *A Church Called Tov: Forming a Goodness Culture That Resists Abuses of Power and Promotes Healing* (Carol Stream, IL: Tyndale House Publishers, 2020); and Diane Langberg, *Redeeming Power: Understanding Authority and Abuse in the Church* (Grand Rapids, MI: Brazos Press, 2020).

[2] N. T. Wright, *Matthew for Everyone*, Part 1, The New Testament for Everyone (Louisville, KY: Westminster John Knox Press, 204), 70.

[3] Dallas Willard, *The Divine Conspiracy: Rediscovering Our Hidden Life in God* (New York: HarperCollins, 2014), 228-30. Emphasis is Willard's, and the insights that follow come largely from Willard.

[4] See https://centerfjp.org.

[5] See https://inthecoracle.org.

[6] "About," Coracle, https://inthecoracle.org/about/#mission.

## 9. WHY IS CONSISTENT SPIRITUAL GROWTH SO DIFFICULT?

[1] Dallas Willard, *Renovation of the Heart: Putting on the Character of Christ* (Colorado Springs, CO: NavPress, 2002), 15.

[2] Willard, *Renovation of the Heart*, 18 (emphasis added).

[3] Willard, *Renovation of the Heart*, 17.

[4] Willard, *Renovation of the Heart*, 14.

[5] N. T. Wright, *Matthew for Everyone*, Part 1, The New Testament for Everyone (Louisville, KY: Westminster John Knox Press, 2004), 193.

[6] Ben Meyer, *The Aims of Jesus*, Princeton Theological Monograph Series, vol. 48 (Eugene, OR: Pickwick Publications, 2002), 110.

[7] Meyer, *The Aims of Jesus*, 141.

[8] Scot McKnight, "Beyond Deconstructionism: Third Term," *Scot's Newsletter*, October 21, 2021, https://scotmcknight.substack.com/p/beyond -deconstruction-third-term.

[9] McKnight, "Beyond Deconstructionism."

## 10. IS THERE AN AUTHENTIC COMMUNITY OF FAITH?

[1] For a deeper understanding of liturgy as a spiritual practice, see my *Giving Church Another Chance: Finding New Meaning in Spiritual Practices* (Downers Grove, IL: InterVarsity Press, 2010).

[2] Ben Meyer, *The Aims of Jesus*, Princeton Theological Monograph Series (Eugene, OR: Pickwick Publications, 2002), 159.

[3] Meyer, *The Aims of Jesus*, 161.

⁴Meyer, *The Aims of Jesus*, 148.

⁵N. T. Wright, *Christian Origins and the Question of God: Jesus and the Victory of God* (Minneapolis: Fortress Press, 1997), 149.

⁶Meyer, *The Aims of Jesus*, 172.

⁷Andy Crouch, *Strong and Weak: Embracing a Life of Love, Risk and True Flourishing* (Downers Grove, IL: InterVarsity Press, 2016), 48.

⁸N. T. Wright, *Simply Christian* (San Francisco, CA: HarperSanFrancisco, 2006), 204.

⁹N. T. Wright, *Evil and the Justice of God* (Downers Grove, IL: InterVarsity Press, 2006), 99.

¹⁰Wright, *Evil and the Justice of God*, 98.

¹¹Dallas Willard, *The Divine Conspiracy: Rediscovering Our Hidden Life in God* (New York: HarperCollins, 2014), 21.

¹²Willard, *The Divine Conspiracy*, 22.

¹³Willard, *The Divine Conspiracy*, 77.

¹⁴Willard, *The Divine Conspiracy*, 67.

¹⁵See Elizabeth O'Connor, *Journey Inward, Journey Outward* (Washington, DC: Potter's House Bookservice, 1968).

¹⁶See Elizabeth O'Connor, *Servant Leaders, Servant Structures* (Washington, DC: Potter's House Bookservice, 1991).

¹⁷See Elizabeth O'Connor, *Call to Commitment* (New York: Harper and Row, 1963). See also Elizabeth O'Connor, *Cry Pain, Cry Hope: A Guide to the Dimensions of Call* (Nashville, TN: Word Books, 1987).

¹⁸See Elizabeth O'Connor, *The Eighth Day of Creation: Gifts and Creativity* (Nashville, TN: Word Books, 1971).

## 11. DO MY RELIGIOUS RESERVATIONS AND CHURCHLY HESITATIONS DISQUALIFY ME?

¹Frederick Buechner, *The Alphabet of Grace* (New York: HarperCollins, 1970), 47.

²Ben Meyer, *The Aims of Jesus*, Princeton Theological Monograph Series (Eugene, OR: Pickwick Publications, 2002), 139.

³Meyer, *The Aims of Jesus*, 147.

⁴Meyer, *The Aims of Jesus*, 137.

⁵Meyer, *The Aims of Jesus*, 151 (emphasis added).

⁶Meyer, *The Aims of Jesus*, 137.

⁷Meyer, *The Aims of Jesus*, 145.

⁸Ranier Maria Rilke, *Letters to a Young Poet*, trans. M. D. Herter Norton (New York: Norton, 2004), 21.

9 See Jack W. Niewold, "Set Theory and Leadership: Reflections on Missional Communities in the Light of Ephesians 4:11-12," *Journal of Biblical Perspectives in Leadership* 2, no. 1 (Winter 2008): 44-63, www.regent .edu/acad/global/publications/jbpl/vol2no1/Niewold_Jack_Final.pdf; Alexander F. Venter, "Social Set Theory (Centered-Set) in Doing Church," July 25, 2018, https://alexanderventer.com/social-set-theory-centered -set-in-doing-church/; "Bounded Set vs. Centered Set Thinking," *Veritas* blog, March 13, 2013, https://veritas.community/veritas-community /2013/03/13/bounded-set-vs-centered-set-thinking.

10 Howard Thurman, *Jesus and the Disinherited* (Boston, MA: Beacon Press, 1996), 19.

# ALSO AVAILABLE

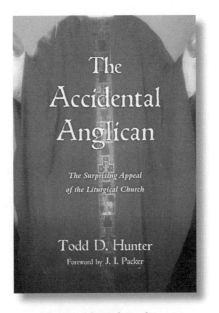

*The Accidental Anglican*
978-0-8308-3839-4